Get Started in Cantonese

Jacqueline Lam

Contents

Acknowledgements

The moment I saw the light at the end of my tunnel, John Donne's famous words came to mind. A twisted version: *No lass is an island, entire of herself.*

This book would not have existed without the 'as a matter of fact' encouragement of Florence Lam and Tom McArthur.

This book would not have existed without Aslan Lam's efficient and effective responses to my questions regarding **Gwóng-dūng-wá** (Cantonese).

This book would not have existed if Sarah Cole, Editorial Director of Hodder Education, had not approached me, and without the professional support of her team, Morven Dooner, Melissa Baker, and Alison Macaulay, my Development Editor, whose ability in picking up a new language can only be described by 'wow!'. At this point, I cannot miss out John Dove and Martin Manser, both of whom indirectly and directly drew my attention to a publishing house that I would have otherwise missed.

Also important are K K Luk and Amy Tsang Wai-lan, who commented on the sets of Cantonese romanization, Allen Ng, who came to the rescue whenever constant internet raids put my computers under threat, and Joey Lam and Alfred Lam, who equipped me with the mobile technology.

This small offering is an interim report of a long research dictionary project, which started in 2002 in Hong Kong, and my gratitude also to Pun Siu-kau and Li Lan. Both have been walking with me on this strenuous journey since then.

Paradoxically, English is also a means of presenting Cantonese to the world. We are experiencing 'the fifth communicative shifts', the advance of the internet, the computer and the mobile phone – the world has almost become one country. Here in Cambridge, I am well connected with all these lovely people in London, Scotland, Hong Kong, Singapore, and Poland through my various computers and tablets: an amusing and amazing business.

For this mission impossible, I am in debt to you all!

Meet the author

Jacqueline Lam 林錦薇 *Làhm Gám·mèih* was born in Hong Kong, growing up with Cantonese, English, Fujianese/Hokkien, Hakka/Hoklo, Chaozhou, and Mandarin/Putonghua. Under the influence of her doctoral supervisor, Reinhard Hartmann, at the University of Exeter, and her husband Tom McArthur, her interest in Cantonese has flourished, whence this book.

A Fellow of the Institute of Linguists, Jacqui is now living in Cambridge after fourteen years of teaching English at the Language Centre of the Hong Kong University of Science and Technology (HKUST). She has been a language consultant since 2007, working as a language teacher and examiner (English, Cantonese, Mandarin/Putonghua), a translator and interpreter, an editor and writer, and a tourist guide for organizations such as the Institute of Linguists, the Foreign Office, Oxford University Press, Cambridge City Council, and Visit Cambridge.

Introduction

Welcome to *Get Started in Cantonese*! This new course has been designed for complete beginners as well as those who, having done a general Cantonese course elsewhere, now wish to learn the language used in Hong Kong, Macau, and South China.

Acquiring a new language is never a simple task, and there is no easy way to become proficient except by constantly exposing oneself to the target language and by using it as much as possible.

This, however, doesn't mean that one cannot be good at a language without living in its place of origin. This is because the impact of advanced technology on communication is profound: easy access to songs, television programmes, films, and videos produced by different countries has lifted the geographical language barrier. I have had the great fortune of meeting a good example in Cambridge – a Chinese scholar who spoke impeccable RP (received pronunciation), yet, in her forty-something years' existence, she had travelled outside China only to the United Kingdom and Australia separately for six months in all. Her secret weapon has been listening to broadcasts, language recordings, films, and videos in the target language. An amusing benefit is that she could choose whatever language model she preferred – in her case, the RP pronunciation.

So, coming back to our target language – Cantonese. There are ample examples of canto-pop and Cantonese films to provide you with the right language environment. Most of all, such supportive learning materials as books, recordings, and dictionaries are plentiful. And indeed, for this reason, in this book, we have chosen the Yale romanization system to guide you through the pronunciation of **Gwóng-dūng-wá**.

Happy learning! **Hòhk-jaahp yuh-faai!**

How the book works

There are ten units in *Get Started in Cantonese*. Each unit has the same basic structure:

What you will learn sets the learning objectives for the unit. At the end of the unit, in the **Self-check** section, you will be given the opportunity to reflect on what you have set out to achieve.

Culture point is a short opening passage in English that introduces the theme of the unit, tells you something about the culture, and introduces some key words and phrases in Cantonese. A question at the end alerts you to some salient points in the text and encourages you to start discovering the language.

Vocabulary builder introduces the essential vocabulary items that you will need to learn in a particular theme. Look at the word lists, complete the missing English meanings, then listen to the accompanying audio and try to imitate the speakers.

New expressions are key phrases and expressions in the unit with their English translations, accompanied by audio. These are the nuts and bolts of the language, so should be priorities for your learning.

Conversation 1 provides a scenario where day-to-day Cantonese from the **Vocabulary builder** is presented both in the text and on the audio. First, read the background information, which sets the scene for what you are going to hear and read. An opening question focuses your attention on a particular point in the dialogue. Further questions after the conversation help you check your comprehension. You can also practise taking the part of one of the speakers in a listen and repeat activity.

Language discovery introduces the key language points in **Conversation 1**. Look for the icon for questions that lead you to discover how the grammar and vocabulary of Cantonese work. Explanations are brief and simple to understand.

Learn more provides further information on some key language points. Read the notes and look back at **Conversation 1** to see how the language has been used.

Practice includes a number of exercises of various types designed to give you the chance to put the new language points into practice, and to help you to start speaking Cantonese in simple situations.

Listen and understand contains sets of listening activities and follow-up questions that will help you increase your capacity to understand spoken Cantonese. Most of the exercises include brief dialogues which appear on the audio but not on the page, mirroring the real-life experience of speaking and understanding a foreign language. Tune up your ears!

Conversation 2 refines the unit theme, introducing additional language, which is explained in the subsequent **Language discovery** and **Learn more** sections.

Speaking provides exercises to help you consolidate what you have learned in the unit and sometimes to recycle language from previous units. To make sure that you have learnt the essentials, try to repeat the exercises as many times as you can until you can 'speak' the lines without referring back to the cues.

Reading contains vocabulary items from the unit and occasional new words. Try getting to know a few Chinese characters and the gist of the text (if there is any) before you answer the follow-up questions. Again, remember that acquiring a new language takes time, so revisit these exercises from time to time.

Writing is a difficult skill in learning the Chinese language. Two writing systems co-exist in the Chinese-speaking world(s): traditional characters, which are still used in such places as Hong Kong, Macau, and Taiwan, and simplified characters, which are used in the PRC, Singapore, and Malaysia. Traditional characters are assets of Chinese culture. Without being well acquainted with them, one cannot fully appreciate the treasures of the civilization developed by our ancestors some 5,000 years ago. However, because of its complexity, writing in Chinese characters is largely beyond the scope of this book. In some units, we have omitted the writing section to prevent overloading you at this stage in your learning. However, in most units there is a short writing section to help you to recognize some useful Chinese characters, and to learn a little about how the characters are formed.

As regards simplified characters, because of the sheer number of people in the PRC of China using them, we have also included them in this course where appropriate. One needs, however, to bear in mind that simplified characters were being used by individuals for decades well before they were standardized in the 1970s. They are not necessarily easier to learn, and at times, can indeed be confusing.

If you like writing, Chinese calligraphy is an art not to be missed. The brushes, ink-sticks, ink-stones, and even the writing papers add to its mystique. It helps you to focus the mind and can be regarded as a kind of yoga in the Chinese domain – endurance and patience are the key. So, go for it!

Go further, **Language tip** and **More vocabulary** introduce more useful words and expressions related to the unit theme and give you handy hints to help you with your learning.

Your turn gives you instant opportunities for practice immediately after what you have just learnt.

Don't forget is a gentle reminder to refresh your memory of what you have learnt previously.

Test yourself sections at the end of each unit help you assess how much you have learnt. When you are ready, work through the tests without referring back to the language notes. If you don't score well the first time, don't be discouraged. Try again and again, and again – you will get there!

Self-check summarizes what you should have learnt in the unit. When you feel that you have understood and practised all of these points, move on to the next unit.

Move through the units in your own time. Think of how you learn your mother tongue – listening is the key, so make good use of the audio to help your learning!

This book also contains various reference sections to help you with your learning:

The **Pronunciation guide** is an overview of Cantonese sounds. For many learners, this is a daunting part of learning Chinese languages, so this section precedes the units. This will allow you to learn a little about Cantonese pronunciation before you start, but I encourage you to go over it from time to time to remind yourself of the various points covered. The more familiar you become with the sounds and tones of Cantonese, the easier it will become to produce them yourself!

Review units appear three times through the book (after Units 3, 6, and 10) to help you consolidate and remember the language you have learnt over several units. Everything you need to answer the review questions has been presented previously. Checking your score will let you know if you are ready to move ahead to new material or if you ought to go back and review your learning. Again, don't be discouraged if you don't get a high score the first time. Practice makes perfect!

Answer key includes the answers to all the activities in the course, including the review units, to allow you to check your work.

Cantonese–English vocabulary. The glossary at the end of the book allows you to look up all the vocabulary that is presented in the course, and maybe more!

To make your learning easier and more efficient, a system of icons indicates the actions you should take:

 Culture tip

Figure something out for yourself

Play the audio track

Listen and pronounce

Exercises – your turn to practise!

New words and phrases

Speak out loud

Reading practice

Have a go at writing

Check your Cantonese ability (be honest with yourself!)

Learn to learn

The Discovery method!

There are lots of philosophies and approaches to language learning, some practical, some quite unconventional, and far too many to list here. Perhaps you know of a few, or even have some techniques of your own. In this book we have incorporated the **Discovery method** of learning, a sort of DIY (do-it-yourself) approach to language learning. What this means is that you will be encouraged throughout the course to engage your mind and figure out the language for yourself, through identifying patterns, understanding grammar concepts, noticing words that are similar to English, and more. This method promotes *language awareness*, a critical skill in acquiring a new language. As a result of your own efforts, you will be able to better retain what you have learnt, use it with confidence, and, even better, apply those same skills to continuing to learn the language (or, indeed, another one) on your own after you've finished this book.

Everyone can succeed in learning a language – the key is to know how to learn it. Learning is more than just reading or memorizing grammar and vocabulary. It's about being an active learner, learning in real contexts, and, most importantly, using what you've learnt in different situations. Simply put, if you **figure something out for yourself**, you're more likely to understand it. And when you use what you've learnt, you're more likely to remember it.

And because many of the essential but (let's admit it!) dull details, such as grammar rules, are introduced through the **Discovery method**, you'll have more fun while learning. Soon, the language will start to make sense and you'll be relying on your own intuition to construct original sentences *independently*, not just listening and repeating.

Enjoy yourself!

Becoming a proficient Cantonese speaker

Learning a language, especially one that is from a different 'family' of languages from your native language, can be a daunting prospect. However, there are some simple things you can do to become a more effective language learner.

VOCABULARY

There are many tricks to learning vocabulary so that it 'sticks' in your head. As well as using the **Vocabulary builders** and **Cantonese–English Vocabulary** in this book, there are lots of other things you can do to help you:

Keep returning to the vocabulary from previous units as you move through the book, so that you are revisiting and recycling the language already learnt. Always try to say the words out loud as well as listening to them. Some people feel silly doing this, but the best way to learn is by really using the language!

Prioritize your vocabulary learning so that you don't waste time learning non-essential words to begin with. Get hold of a good Cantonese–English dictionary. Every time you come across a new word, make a mark against the relevant entry in the dictionary. When you have three marks next to a word, it's clearly an important word, and so worth spending a little more time learning it until you remember it.

Keep a separate vocabulary book, or a record on your smartphone or tablet device, divided in a way that makes sense to you; A–Z is possible, but thematic groups of words may be more memorable.

Many people use mind maps and flash cards to help them learn new words, or make stickers for objects around the house with the Cantonese name for the object on them.

Make good use of 'real life' language: modern technology makes this so much easier! Listen to Cantonese radio stations, watch television or films in the language, and make use of apps on such mobile technology as smartphones. Do songs interest you? There are many Cantonese songs available to listen to and view on the internet. You might even learn a few by listening to CDs or DVDs and by singing karaoke.

Look for patterns in words, for example, adding **hóu** to an adjective means *very*, so **hóu-hóu** is *very good*, **hóu-leng** is *very pretty*, **hóu-chìh** is *very late*.

Above all – USE the language!

GRAMMAR

Grammar in Cantonese may seem frightening, but in many ways, it is much simpler than in English and there are relatively few rules to learn – you'll learn more about this as you go through the book.

Look for examples of grammar patterns you learn in the book as you explore Cantonese in the real world (for example in magazines or when watching films).

See how the rules you learn compare to the rules of English and any other languages you know. Sometimes they will be similar, and sometimes very different.

Once again, practice makes perfect, so keep trying to apply what you learn to your spoken Cantonese.

SPEAKING

People who learn a new language often find that what they 'know' from classes or a book vanishes as soon as they open their mouth to have a conversation in that language.

There are lots of opportunitites in the book to practise speaking, using the conversations and other listening and speaking exercises. Try to repeat these often to get into the habit of speaking in Cantonese, and also try to say the answers to other questions and exercises out loud for further practice.

Look for opportunities to speak Cantonese in the real world. Perhaps your local college or university has a Cantonese-speaking student who might do a 'language swap' with you (for example, half an hour speaking English, half an hour speaking Cantonese once a week). Perhaps if you go to a restaurant with Cantonese-speaking staff, you could try ordering your food in Cantonese!

When you are on your own, try naming the objects around you out loud, or rehearsing conversations in Cantonese.

Don't worry about making mistakes; it's a natural part of language learning. In Cantonese, even if you make some mistakes with the tone of a word, your listener will figure out what you are trying to say from the context. Try to learn from your slip-ups, especially when you find you are making the same mistake over and over again.

Keep things simple to start with. The most important thing is to get your message across. Think of different ways to say something if you're unsure and make use of gestures and even the occasional English word if you have to.

PRONUNCIATION

Speaking and pronunciation go hand-in-hand, and it can be hard to perfect pronunciation on your own. However, there are some things you can do to help.

If possible, record yourself reading the conversations and other audio material in the book, and then compare this with the audio. Many electronic devices will allow you to do this. What sounds are very different when you compare the audio?

Keep a note of any sounds or tones that you find difficult and return to them often.

Pay particular attention to aspects of pronunciation that are very different from English, such as tones.

LISTENING

When the native speaker you are talking to doesn't use the phrase you expect in an answer, or speaks very quickly, it can cause blind panic! Listening is a difficult skill to master, but it's a very important one, so make good use of the recorded material in the book to help you develop your listening skills.

Think about different ways in which a question might be answered. There is often more than one possible answer to a question, so be prepared for different possibilities.

Try not to worry if you don't catch every word of what a speaker is saying. In many situations, understanding the gist is more important than understanding every individual word, and will allow you to communicate effectively. As your confidence and experience improve, so will your ability to understand more of what is being said.

Use clues in the context to help you guess the meaning of unknown words. This is also a useful skill to develop when reading.

CRACKING THE CULTURAL MYTH

'Culture' is a big word. As the world has become smaller, because of the advance of science and technology, and international education, an individual's behaviour doesn't necessarily reflect ethnic culture. The basic rule for dealing with Cantonese people, as everywhere else, is to be sincere and be polite. Don't forget to say *thank you*, **m̀h-gōi** (for a service), and **dō-jeh** (when given something). Don't miss out *sorry*, **deui-m̀h-jyuh**, if you don't know whether you are doing or saying the right thing. Try to say those words with a friendly face and an appropriate smile; you will be astonished how helpful Cantonese people can be!

One last word: learn to understand Cantonese rude words and foul language, but don't say them out loud, and definitely not in public.

Useful expressions

GREETINGS, FAREWELLS, AND COURTESIES

hello	**hā-lóu; néih hóu; wái** – on phone
welcome	**fūn-yìhng**
How are you?	**Néih-hóu-maa?; Néih-dím aa?**
I'm fine, thanks, and you?	**Ngóh géi-hóu/hóu-hóu, néih nē?**
long time no see	**hóu-noih móuh-gin**
What's your name?	**Néih giu māt-méng aa?** (informal)
	Néih dím-chīngfù aa? (formal)
My name is . . .	**Ngóh giu-jouh . . .**
Pleased to meet you.	**Hóu hòi-sàm gin-dóu-néih;**
	Hóu gōu-hing yìhng-sīk néih.
good morning	**jóu-sàhn**
good afternoon	**ńgh-ōn**
good evening	**máahn-ōn** (culturally, Cantonese seldom say good evening to each other)
good night	**jóu-táu**
goodbye	**joi-gin** (formal); **bāai-baai** (informal)
good luck	**jūk-néih hóu-wahn**
bon voyage	**yāt-louh seuhn-fùng**
	yāt-louh pìhng-ngòn
excuse me	**chéng-mahn** – to get attention
	m̀hgòi – to get past
	sàt-pùih – used when leaving for a while
sorry	**deui-m̀h-jyuh**
thank you	**dòjeh** – for a gift; **m̀hgòi** – for a service
response to thank you	**m̀h-sái haak-hei** – don't mention it;
	móuh mahntàih – no problem
get well soon	**jóu-yaht hōng-fuhk** (formal);
	faaidi hóufàan aa (informal)

MAKING YOURSELF UNDERSTOOD

Do you speak English?	**Néih sihk-m̀h-sihk gwóng yīng-mán aa?**
Could you please speak more slowly?	**Néih hó-m̀h-hó-yi gwóng-maahn-dī aa?**
Sorry, what did you say?	**Deui-m̀h-jyuh, néih gwóng mē-aa?**
Sorry, I don't understand.	**Deui-m̀h-jyuh, nógh tēng-m̀h chīng-chó.**
Could you please repeat?	**M̀h-goi joi-gwóng yāt-chi.**

NECESSITIES

Where's the toilet?	**Chi-só hái bīn-douh aa?** (informal);
	Sái-sáu-gāan hái bīn-douh aa? (formal)
How much (is this)?	**(Nī-go) géi-dō chín aa?**
The bill, please.	**M̀h-goi màaih-dāan!**
I love you.	**Ngóh-oi-néih.**

NUMBERS

1 **yāt**	11 **sahp-yāt**	21 **yih-sahp-yāt**	40 **sei-sahp**
2 **yih**	12 **sahp-yih**	22 **yih-sahp-yih**	50 **ǹgh-sahp**
3 **sāam**	13 **sahp-sām**	23 **yih-sahp-sāam**	60 **luhk-sahp**
4 **sei**	14 **sahp-sei**	24 **yih-sahp-sei**	70 **chāt-sahp**
5 **ńgh**	15 **sahp-ńgh**	25 **yih-sahp-ńgh**	80 **baat-sahp**
6 **luhk**	16 **sahp-luhk**	26 **yih-sahp-luhk**	90 **gáu-sahp**
7 **chāt**	17 **sahp-chāt**	27 **yih-sahp-chāt**	100 **yāt-baak**
8 **baat**	18 **sahp-baat**	28 **yih-sahp-baat**	1,000 **yāt-chīn**
9 **gáu**	19 **sahp-gáu**	29 **yih-sahp-gáu**	100,000 **sahp-maahn**
10 **sahp**	20 **yih-sahp**	30 **sāam-sahp**	1,000,000 **yāt-baak-maahn**

0 is **lihng** and 1,000,000,000 is **sahp-yīk** (literally *a hundred million*).
More information can be found in Units 1, 2, 3 in this book and the *Complete Cantonese* book by the same publisher.

QUESTION WORDS

Where?	**Bīn-douh?**
Where?	**Heui-bīn-douh?**
How?	**Dím-yéung?**
Why?	**Dím-gáai?**
When?	**Géi-sìh?**
How much?; How many?	**Géi-dō?**
Which? Who?	**Bīn-go?**
What?	**Mē-yéh?; Māt-yéh?**

Pronunciation guide

This book uses a system known as romanization to indicate the sound of Cantonese. By 'translating' Chinese characters into a Roman alphabet, speakers of languages which use such an alphabet will find it easier to gain access to the language. Cantonese children learn Cantonese by listening to people around them. They do not learn the sounds through romanization. For foreigners, especially those who have not been in touch with Cantonese speakers, romanization is a gateway to Cantonese sounds on paper. Hence, learning can be more free from social and geographical constraints.

The Yale romanization system

Four Yale romanization systems were created at Yale University for romanizing four East Asian languages: Mandarin, Cantonese, Korean, and Japanese. In recent years, *Hanyu pinyin* (a romanization system used by the People's Republic of China for Putonghua, a variant of Mandarin) has largely superseded the Yale system for Mandarin, but the Yale romanization system for Cantonese remains the most popular way of presenting Cantonese in the Roman alphabet, and is the system used in this book.

The Yale romanization used in this book

In order to help learners to start Cantonese with confidence, in this book, we have slightly adapted the original Cantonese Yale. In terms of the number of tones, and the use of **aa** to denote the longer **a** vowel whenever necessary as in names like **aa-Fān**, **aa-Wàih**, and **aa-Lìhng** and such sentence-final particles as **maa**.

SYLLABLES

Each Chinese character is represented by a syllable of the Cantonese Yale. Each syllable is composed of three elements: *initial, final,* and *tone*. An example of the syllable 我 (*I*) is presented on the right:

Tone mark

Ngóh   我 (*I*)

Initial   Finals

(see Hung, 1996)[1]

---

[1] Hung, B. (1996) *Phrases in Cantonese*. Hong Kong: Greenwood Press.

Initials

These are the beginning sound element of a syllable, and there are 19 in total. The first ten introduced here come in pairs. Although examples are given, they should be for reference only. In order to become proficient in the language, listening to the sounds is the key.

Aspirated
examples in English (RP)
p as in *papa*
t as in *tap*
ch as in *chacha*
k as in *kola/cola-nut*
kw as in *quite*

Unaspirated
examples in English (RP)
b as in *bill*
d as in *dog*
j as in *gypsy* (somewhere between *ts* in *cats* and *tch* in *catch*)
g as in *get*
gw as in *language*

The remaining nine syllables are more or less similar to those in English:

f	as in *far*
h	as in *hat*
l	as in *leg*
m	as in *man* (nasal)
n	as in *now* (nasal)
ng	as in *singing* (nasal)
s	as in *see*
w	as in *wet*
y	as in *yes*

Finals

These are the ending sound element of a syllable. There are 51 in total (as **a** and **aa** are customarily counted as one).

a	aa	e	eu	i	o	u	yu
ak	aak	ek	euk	ik	ok	uk	
am	aam			im			
an	aan		eun	in	on	un	yun
ang	aang	eng	eung	ing	ong	ung	
ap	aap			ip			
at	aat		eut	it	ot	ut	yut
ai	aai	ei	eui		oi	ui	
au	aau			iu	ou		

Putting the 19 initials and 51 finals together, we have about 590 possible Cantonese sounds. Finals are the combination of consonants and vowels.

When two or more vowels stick together, the technical name for them is diphthong. Here is a brief description of how consonants, vowels, and diphthongs work in Cantonese 'finals'. For details, please refer to *Complete Cantonese*.

Consonants: only six of them, **-n**, **-ng**, **-m**, **-p**, **-t**, and **-k**, appear at the end of Cantonese syllables. The first three are similar to English, but when **p**, **t**, and **k** are at the end of the syllables, they are hardly pronounced at all. The effect resembles the English 'glottal stop' as in '*put your ha? on*'.

Vowels: including both **-a** and **-aa**, there are eight vowels in Cantonese. They are:

-a	as in the southern English pronunciation of *but*
-aa	is a longer version of the **a** sound. In the Yale system, if there is no final consonant, it is represented with just one **a**.
-e	as in *ten*
-eu	as in *her*; similar to the French *eu* (as in *feu*), or the German *ö* (as in *schön*)
-i	as in *bee*, similar to long /i:/ in IPA
-o	as in *oral*
-u	as in *fool*
-yu	as in *deep*, but with the lips rounded; similar to the French *u* (as in *tu*), or the German *ü* (as in *Tür*)

Diphthongs: consist of the vowels in different combinations, and there are nine of them in total:

ai	the combination of **a** and **i**, a very short diphthong, as in *kite*
au	the combination of **a** and **u**, as in *out*
aai	the combination of **aa** and **i**, as in *lie*
aau	the combination of **aa** and **u**, as in *owl*
eui	the combination of **eu** and **i**, as in '*he? dress*' (without pronouncing *r*)
iu	the combination of **i** and **u**, as in *seal*
oi	the combination of **o** and **i**, as in *boy*
ou	the combination of **o** and **u**, as in *toe*
ui	the combination of **u** and **i**, sounds like *oo-ey*, as in *phooey*.

For more practice on the sounds of consonants, vowels, and diphthongs, please refer to *Complete Cantonese*.

WORD DIVISION

Primarily, each Chinese character is represented by one syllable and characters are written one at a time discretely (i.e. characters are never 'joined up' as letters are in English). So, when words are transcribed into Cantonese Yale, they are also written discretely one after the other with a space in between. However, as in English, in speech, Cantonese people do not utter the monosyllabic words one at a time because that would sound robotic. This is especially true in the Cantonese language because Cantonese syllables carry (almost) equal stress. Good utterances should flow like water.

To achieve such an effect, the Committee for Language Reform of China (CLRC) recommends, in the *Basic Rules for Hanyu Pinyin Orthography*, putting multi-syllabic words together so as to form meaningful compound Chinese words. In order to make the texts clearer to beginners, instead of putting the same group of words into one single item, in this book we use hyphens to indicate both their continuity and uniqueness. So the sentence **Giu ngòh Wòhng táai lā!** (*Call me Mrs Wong!*) becomes **Giu-ngòh Wòhng-táai lā!** (and not, for example, **Giungòh Wòhngtáai lā!*) For teaching purposes, how the words are hyphenated varies from unit to unit. In the early units, two or three words are joined together to identify a single concept. In the later units, more words will be hyphenated to form a longer string, matching authentic Cantonese speech.

TONE

Cantonese is a tonal language. The relative pitch at which a syllable is pronounced distinguishes one word from another. The change of tone in a word will automatically change the meaning of that word, and sometimes the outcome can be hilarious. Fortunately, it is still possible to understand speakers' intentions in context even if one or two tones are not 'properly' pitched.

Tone is part of the beautiful Cantonese language, but it can be, at times, a physical as well as psychological barrier, especially for adult learners. Many scholars compare the Cantonese tones to singing songs. Some learners find the musical analogy helpful. In this respect, we encourage you to choose a word (from the list of examples given), memorize its different tones in sequence, and 'sing' them out as frequently as you can until you get the grip of their sounds in your head. As a native Cantonese speaker, I learnt to assign the tone-values to my Cantonese in my very late adulthood (because Cantonese romanization has never been part of

---

* denotes wrongly constructed phrase/sentence

the school syllabus. As a child, we were taught to associate the Cantonese sound with Chinese characters only). So with some determination and patience, acquiring the tones is not as difficult as people generally expect.

How many tones?

There are many schools of thought regarding the number of Cantonese tones, which in effect vary according to regions, but it is probably between six and ten. Beginners, however, can get by with six, and that is more or less all that outsiders can identify in Hong Kong people's speech. To help you start, in this book, we will settle with the six most recognizable tone levels. They are the levels of high, mid-rising, mid, low-falling, low-rising, and low, as illustrated below:

HIGH	MID-RISING	MID	LOW-FALLING	LOW-RISING	LOW
1st tone	2nd tone	3rd tone	4th tone	5th tone	6th tone
(high)	(low-mid → high)	(mid)	(mid-low → low)	(mid-low → mid)	(mid-low)

A graphic representation of the pitch contours of the six Cantonese tones

In Cantonese Yale, the six levels are identified by three diacritic marks, the acute (´), the grave (`), and the macron (¯), together with the letter **h**, which denotes low tones. The vowel **o** is used for illustration below:

	Rising	Level	Falling
High	ō (1st tone)		
	ó (2nd tone)		
Mid	o (3rd tone)		
Mid-low	óh (5th tone)	oh (6th tone)	òh (4th tone)
Low			

Notes of caution:

1 **h** is a tonal symbol indicating low tones when it is not the first letter of a syllable. It should not be pronounced (similar to the syllable-end consonants **p**, **t**, and **k** already mentioned). It might take some time to get used to this idea, but eventually it will stick. So, be patient with the symbol!

2 In some publications, you might see the use of symbol high-falling at work, as in **gàm-yaht** (*today*), because the original Cantonese Yale embraces seven tones. One can however pronounce the word as **gām-yaht** (with **gām** in the first tone) and, happily, discover that nobody even notices the difference. Most native Cantonese people would not be aware of the change of the high-level to the high-falling tone. This is especially true among youngsters.

Practice

 00.01

1 **Listen to the following four examples carefully to distinguish the six tones of each syllable.**

 00.02

2 **Now listen to each sound and imitate the speaker as closely as you can.**

 00.03

3 **Imagine that they are lines of lyrics, and try to 'sing' them out loud.**

Tone	HIGH	MID-RISING	MID	LOW-FALLING	LOW-RISING	LOW
Romanization	**fān**	**fán**	**fan**	**fàhn**	**fáhn**	**fahn**
Chinese character	分	粉	瞓	墳	奮	份
English translation	*split*	*powder*	*sleep*	*grave*	*arouse*	*portion*
Romanization	**fū**	**fú**	**fu**	**fùh**	**fúh**	**fuh**
Chinese character	呼	苦	褲	扶	婦	父
English translation	*call*	*bitter*	*trousers*	*support*	*woman*	*father*
Romanization	**sī**	**sí**	**si**	**sìh**	**síh**	**sih**
Chinese character	詩	史	試	時	市	是
English translation	*poem*	*history*	*try*	*time*	*market*	*matter*
Romanization	**yāu**	**yáu**	**yau**	**yàuh**	**yáuh**	**yauh**
Chinese character	休	柚	幼	游	有	又
English translation	*rest*	*pomelo†*	*young*	*swim*	*have*	*again*

† A kind of fruit common in Asia.

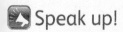 Speak up!

1 When you are confident enough, 'sing' each line out loud, then listen to the audio of the same line and check whether you have got that line correct. At this point, you can also record your own utterance, and compare your pronunciation with those on the audio.

2 Select one of syllables you like in the list, and practise the six tones of that particular syllable until they are imprinted in your mind.

3 When you can remember the six tones of your selected syllable by heart, you can now transfer the 'melody' onto any syllable you pick. This is how you acquire the skill of identifying the tone of a Cantonese word.

4 When you are ready, 'sing' the following words in six tones. Don't worry that some of the tones do not have corresponding Cantonese characters.

a	bā	bá	ba	bàh	báh	bah
b	chīn	chín	chin	chìhn	____	____
c	dāa	dáa	da	____	____	____
d	mā	má	____	____	____	____
e	fā	____	____	____	____	____

你好! *Néih-hóu!*

Hello!

In this unit you will learn how to:
▶ *say hello and goodbye.*
▶ *introduce yourself and others.*

CEFR (A1): *Can understand and use basic phrases for greetings, farewells, and introduce oneself and others.*

廣東話 Gwóng-dūng-wá *Cantonese*

Gwóng-dūng-wá (*Cantonese*) is what **Gwóng-dūng-yahn** (*Cantonese people*) speak. The language originates in the province of Canton, and is broadly known as **Gwóng-jāu-wá**, *the speech of Guangzhou*, the capital of East Canton in China. In the past half century, the language has been kept alive in Hong Kong by the population at large, the media, and popular entertainments. The mix of Eastern and Western culture in Hong Kong has enriched the language. In the 16th century, Cantonese served as the basis of Pidgin English, which for centuries helped promote trade and business between the world and South China.

Cantonese is highly colloquial and its people vibrant and creative: they like to pun, and to have fun with language. The language also reflects their strong sense of identity, and is often written in a traditional set of Chinese characters with distinct meanings from the norm.

Despite the recent enthusiasm for learning **gwok-yúh** (*Mandarin*) or **póu-tūng-wá** (*Putonghua*), as it is also known, Cantonese remains one of the most widely spoken Chinese languages worldwide. As well as being used by over 80 million people in the southern province of Canton (East and West), **Hēung-góng** (*Hong Kong*) and **Ou-mún** (*Macau*), it is also widely spoken outside **Jūng-gwok** (*China*), in South-East Asia, in such places as Indonesia, Malaysia, and Singapore. In the late 20th century, a vast migration of Cantonese speakers to Australia, Canada, New Zealand, **Yīng-gwok** (*the United Kingdom*), and **Méih-gwok** (*the United States*) has extended the spread of Cantonese as a *lingua franca* among those Chinese communities abroad.

1 What do you call Cantonese people in the Cantonese language?

2 What do you think **gwok** means in the text?.

Vocabulary builder

01.01 Complete the missing English expressions, then listen to the audio and try to imitate the speakers as closely as you can.

介紹 *GAAI-SIUH* FORMAL GREETINGS

哈囉（你好）	hāa-lóu (nèih-hóu)	hello/_____ there! (literally *Hello, you good*)
早晨	jóu-sàhn	*good morning*
你好嗎？	Néih-hóu-maa?	*How are _____?*
我好好	Ngóh-hóu-hóu.	*I am very well.*
幾好	géi-hóu	*quite well/not too bad*
你呢？	Néih-nē?	*What about you?*
多謝	dō-jeh	*thank you* (for a gift)

生詞 *SĀANG-CHÌH* NEW EXPRESSIONS

你	néih	*you*
我	ngóh	*I*
都	dōu	*also*
請問	Chíng-mahn . . .	*May (I) ask . . .*
貴姓？	Gwai-sing?	*What is your name?* (formal)
我姓	Ngóh-sing . . .	*My surname is . . .*
李	Lèih	*Lee* (an Anglicized Chinese surname)
陳	Chàhn	*Chan* (an Anglicized Chinese surname)
先生	sīn-sāng	*Mr*
小姐	síu-jé	*Miss*
吖	āa	particle: *agreeing*
我嚟介紹	Ngóh làih gaai-siuh . . .	*Let me introduce . . .*
呢位係...	Nēi-wái haih . . .	*This is . . .*
點稱呼	Dím chīng-fū?	*What's your name?* (literally *How should I call you?*)
叫我..., 　我叫...	giu-ngóh . . . , 　ngóh-giu . . .	*call me . . . , I am called . . .*

Bowing

It has been quite a long time since Chinese people bowed to each other in greeting. People only do that for fun now – this is also true of putting two palms together as if praying. For friends, the Chinese will say **hāa-lóu** *hello* or **néih-hóu**, and may wave to each other. In business, the most common way of greeting someone is to shake hands. Hugging is extremely rare, as is kissing on the cheeks. Smiles from a woman are simply a sign of politeness and friendliness – don't mistake it as having further implications! Touching is an absolute taboo, unless you know the person really well.

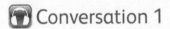 Conversation 1

01.02 At an international wine-tasting reception in Hong Kong, Arthur Chi-wai introduces himself to Jennifer Sam-yi, who is also attending. Listen and complete the exercises that follow.

1 What are the surnames of Arthur Chi-wai and Jennifer Sam-yi?
Mr _____ and Miss _____.

Arthur	Néih-hóu.
Jennifer	Néih-hóu, jóu-sàhn!
Arthur	Ngóh-sing-Léih, chíng-máhn gwai-sing?
Jennifer	Ngóh-sing Chàhn.
Arthur	Chàhn síu-jé, néih hóu-maa?
Jennifer	Ngóh hóu-hóu! Néih nē, Léih sīn-sāang?
Arthur	Ngóh dōu géi-hóu āa, m̀h-gōi.

> **LANGUAGE TIP**
> **Hóu** is *good*. When we repeat the word twice to form **hóu-hóu**, the first **hóu** means *very*, and the two-word expression means *very good*.

2 Match the Cantonese and the English.

a	ngóh	**1**	you
b	néih	**2**	good morning
c	jóu-sàhn	**3**	Mr
d	síu-jé	**4**	I
e	sīn-sáang	**5**	Miss

3 Read the conversation again and answer the questions.
  a What does Arthur ask Jennifer to open the conversation? _____
  b What is the Cantonese for *good morning*? _____
  c How does Jennifer say she is? _____
  d How is Arthur? _____
  e What are the responses for *quite good* and *very good*? _____

> **LANGUAGE TIP**
> Don't be surprised if you hear Cantonese people in the street say **góng** rather than **gwóng** in Gwóng-dōng-wá, **léih** instead of **néih** in such expression as **Néi-hóu-maa?**, **o** instead of **ngóh** in **Ngó sing-Chán**, and **chéng-máhn** (*May [I] ask . . .*) instead of **chíng-máhn**. (See *Complete Cantonese* for details.)

4 *01.03* **Listen to Conversation 1 line by line and repeat. Pay attention to the pronunciation. Then listen to Arthur's lines and answer as if you were Jennifer.**

💡 Language discovery 1

1 Look at the first and third lines of Conversation 1, and decide:
   a Which word in **Néi-hóu** refers to *you*?
   b Which word in **Ngó sing-Léih** means *I*?

LEARN MORE – IDENTIFYING PEOPLE AND THINGS

In English, we use the pronouns *I*, *he*, *she*, *it* to identify people and things. This is how we say them in Cantonese:

我	**ngóh**	*I; me*
你	**néih**	*you*
佢	**kéuih**	*he, she; him, her (for people), it (for animals and things)*

Adding **deih** turns singular pronouns into plurals:

我哋	**ngóh-deih**	*we; us*
你哋	**néih-deih**	*you*
佢哋	**kéuih-deih**	*they; them*

🔒 Practice 1

🎤 **1** 01.04 **Listen to the pronunciation of the pronouns, and repeat. When you are confident enough, say the words in Cantonese.**
   a you
   b she
   c we
   d it
   e he
   f they

2 If Ngóh sing-Léih **means** *I am Lee*, **and** Ngóh sing-Chàhn **means** *I am Chan*, **how do you think you might say** *I am Wong*?

🎧 **3** 01.05 **Now reply to the following in Cantonese:**
   a Néih-hóu!
   b Chíng-mahn gwai-sing?
   c Néih-hóu-maa?

Listen and understand

 01.06 In English, while we address men as *Mr*, there are different ways of addressing women. This is the same in Cantonese. Listen to the audio and imitate the pronunciation of the speaker.

先生	sīn-sāang	Mr
太太	taai-táai	Mrs
小姐	síu-jé	Miss
女士	néuih-sih	Ms

 As with *Ms* in English, **néuih-sih** is a respectable way of addressing Chinese women regardless of their marital status. It is, however, used more in formal situations in Chinese society, and is less likely to be used by younger women.

Now try to answer the following questions in Cantonese. Use Conversation 1 to help you:

a How would you address Mr Lee's wife?

b How would you address Mrs Chan's husband?

c How would you formally address your colleague without indicating her marital status?

d How would you address a female customer whom you know is still single?

> **LANGUAGE TIP**
> The order of addressing a person in Cantonese is: **surname + title**. You will learn more about this in the Take it further section.

Take it further

When we address people in English, we put the titles first. For a man with the surname *Lee*, we call him *Mr Lee*, and a woman either *Mrs*, *Miss*, or *Ms Lee*. However, in Cantonese, all titles, such as *Doctor*, *President*, *Chairman*, *Reverend*, as well as *Mr*, *Mrs*, etc., are put after the surname. So *Mr Lee* becomes **Léih-sīn-sāang** (literally *Lee Mr*), and *Miss Lee* would be **Léih-síu-jé** (*Lee Miss*).

SURNAMES

A recent survey indicates that the top five most common Chinese surnames around the world are **Wong**, **Lee**, **Cheung**, **Lau**, and **Chan**. However, ranking varies as population grows. It also differs regionally. For example, **Chan** ranks fifth globally, but is the biggest family name in Hong Kong, Macau, and Taiwan.

Ten common Chinese surnames (and their English spellings)

王, 黃	**Wòng**	*Wong*		楊	**Jèung**	*Yeung*
李	**Léih**	*Lee/Li*		吳	**Ngh**	*Ng*
張	**Jèung**	*Cheung*		趙	**Jiuh**	*Chiu*
劉	**Làuh**	*Lau*		周	**Jāu**	*Chau*
陳	**Chàhn**	*Chan*		除	**Chùih**	*Tsui*

The *Hundred Family Surnames*, a Chinese classic compiled for children in the Song Dynasty, mentions 504 Chinese family names. It is a rhyme poem with eight surnames in each line. The first four listed in the book, **Chau**, **Chin**, **Suen**, and **Lee**, are said to be the most important families in the empire at the time.

The English spellings of such surnames as **Cheung**, **Lee**, and **Chan** do not necessarily reflect actual Cantonese sounds. Don't worry, though: you will learn how to say them the Cantonese way using the romanization system in this book, in the Vocabulary builder and Conversation sections.

Practice 2

01.07 **Listen to the audio. Number the names in the order you hear them (from 1 to 5). Write the English equivalents of the names. Then listen again and repeat the names, paying attention to pronunciation.**

		Order	In English
a	Jiuh néuih-sih	_____	_____
b	Wòhng sāang	_____	_____
c	Chàhn síu-jé	_____	_____
d	Jāu tai-tái	_____	_____
e	Làuh tái	_____	_____

> **LANGUAGE TIP**
> **Sāang** is short for **sīn-sāang**. **Tái** is short for **tai-tái**.

WHAT ABOUT FORENAMES?

Unlike English names, Cantonese forenames are placed after surnames. Hence, **Chi-wai Lei** becomes **Lee Chi-wai**, and **Sam-yi Chan** is **Chan Sam-yi**. Titles are always placed after forenames. So, *Mr Arthur Lee* becomes *Lee Arthur Mr* (**Léih Arthur sīn-sāang**), and *Miss Jennifer Chan* is *Chan Jennifer Miss* (**Chàhn Jennifer síu-zé**). As with surnames, Chinese forenames can be a single character or two characters. Some common Cantonese forenames are shown in the next exercise.

 Cantonese names can reflect the entwined East–West culture of Hong Kong when, for example, they are written as **Jennifer Chan Sam-yi** or **Arthur Lee Chi-wai**.

 1 01.08 Now listen to the audio, paying attention to the pronunciation. When you're confident enough, say the names out loud.

Female			Male		
心怡	**Sām-yìh**	*Sam-yi*	家豪	**Gāa-hòuh**	*Ka-ho*
佩玲	**Pui-lìhng**	*Pui-ling*	志偉	**Ji-wáih**	*Chi-wai*
淑芬	**Súhk-fān**	*Suk-fan*	俊傑	**Jeun-giht**	*Chun-kit*

> **LANGUAGE TIP**
> Each character in these names can also be used as a single character name, So, **Sām-yìh** can be **Sām** or **Yìh**. We can also put two single characters together to form new names as with **Sām-lìhng** or **Pui-fān**.

Informally, Cantonese people often shorten their names by adding the word **aa** in front of the forenames. If the forename is made up of two characters, **aa** can be added to either of them. One example is in Conversation 2, when Miss Chan calls Mrs Wong **aa-Fān**, a shortened version of **Súhk-Fān**.

 2 01.09 Listen carefully to the audio, and write down the short form of the following names. Then listen again and repeat the names, paying attention to pronunciation.

a Sām-yìh   aa-Yìh
b Gāa-hòuh   aa-_____
c Pui-lìhng   aa-_____
d Ji-wáih   _____
e Súhk-fān   _____
f Jeun-giht   _____

Conversation 2

While Arthur and Jennifer are chatting over a glass of wine, Wong, a colleague of Jennifer, comes up to say hello.

1 **What is Mr Lee's Chinese name?**
2 **Is Wong a man or a woman?**

Wong	*Hi, Jennifer!*
Jennifer	Hi, aa-Fān, ngóh làih gaai-siuh. Nēi wái haih Léih-sāang.
Arthur	Dím chīng-fū aa?
Wong	Giu-ngòh Wòhng-táai lāa!
Arthur	Wòhng-táai, néih-hóu.
Jennifer	Neìh-hóu, Léih-sāang! Nèih giu mē-méng nē?
Arthur	Ngóh-giu aa-Wáih.
Wong	Néih hóu-maa, aa-Wáih?
Arthur	Ngóh géi-hóu, néih-nē?
Wong	Ngóh hóu-hóu.

> **LANGUAGE TIP**
> In the expression **Néih-giu mē-méng** (*What is your name?*), **mē** is short for **mǎt-yéh**, which you might hear people use as in **Néih-giu mǎt-yeh méng?**

3 **Review these expressions from the conversation, then fill in the blanks with the missing English meanings.**

   a Ngóh làih gaai-siuh.   *Let me _____.*
   b Nēi wái haih Lèih-sāang.   *_____ Mr Lee.*
   c Dím cīng-fū aa?   *What should I _____ you?*
   d Giu-ngòh Wòhng-táai lāa!   *_____ Mrs Wong, please.*
   e Nèih giu mē-méng nē?   *What's your _____?*
   f Ngóh-giu aa-Wáih.   *_____ aa-Wai.*
   g Néih hóu-maa?   *_____ are you?*
   h Ngóh hóu-hóu.   *I am _____.*

Language discovery 2

Cantonese people sometimes add some grunts and noises at the end of a sentence. They are usually in the form of a single character. We call these **final particles**.

Here are five lines from both Conversations 1 and 2. Can you identify which word is the final particle?

   a Dím-cīng-fū aa?   aa   d Néih-giu mē-méng-nē? _____
   b Néih-nē?   _____   e Géi-hóu-āa!   _____
   c Giu-ngóh Wòhng-táai lāa! _____

Grunts and noises

You can't translate these end-of-sentence sounds with a single English word, but they can be used for expressing mood, modifying meaning, softening tone, and expressing certain functions. Mastering these little noises shows a good grip of the language, but using them inaccurately could sound funny, odd, or even insulting. It might be wise to learn a few particles at a time, and check their appropriateness with a Cantonese speaker. There are over 100 such particles, and we can start with the 3 used in the Conversations.

Particle	Example	Explanations
aa	1 Dím-chīng-fū aa?	1 used at the end of a question
	2 Dōu géi-hóu aa	2 softens the tone of a statement
āa	Géi-hóu āa	makes a reply sound polite or enthusiastic
lāa	Giu-ngóh Wong-táai lāa!	often used in requests and orders; leaving it out could sound rude
nē	1 Néih-giu mē-méng nē?	1 added at the end of a question, either as a follow-up or a question that does not require an answer
	2 Néih-nē?	2 throws a question back at someone without repeating it, a bit like 'How about you?' in English

 Practice 3

01.11 **Now listen to the lines below, and repeat. Write down those final particles in the blanks.**

a Néih _____?
b Giu-ngóh Wòhng-táai _____!
c Néih-giu mē-méng _____?
d Dím-chīng-fū _____?
e Géi-hóu _____!

1 01.12 **Listen to the conversation and re-arrange it to match the English dialogue, which is in the correct order.**

a Ngóh-giu aa-Tòhng, Dím-chīng-fū aa?

b Aa-Lìhng, néih-hóu-maa?

c Hello! Néih-hóu.

d Ngóh hóu-hóu! Néih-nē, aa-Tòhng?

e Ngóh dōu-géi-hóu āa.

f Ngóh-giu aa-Lìhng.

g Néih-hóu, jóu-sàhn!

1 Hi there, how are you?

2 Hello, good morning.

3 I am aa-Tong. What is your name?

4 I am aa-Ling.

5 Aa-Ling, how are you?

6 I am fine. What about you, aa-Tong?

7 I am quite OK.

2 01.13 **Listen and complete the sentences with the missing words.**

a Ngóh-hóu-hóu, _____?

b Ngóh-sing-Léih, dím _____?

c Ngóh m̀h-haih Jūng-gwok-yàhn, _____?

d Ngóh-sing Chàhn, chíng-máhn _____?

e _____ Méih-gwok-yàhn.

f Léih-sāang, néih-giu _____?

3 How would you say the following in Cantonese?

a What's your name (formal)?

b I'm very well!

c Let me introduce…

d How are you, Miss Chan?

SELF CHECK

I CAN . . .

○ . . . say hello and goodbye.

○ . . . introduce myself and others.

2 我係邊個? *Ngóh-haih bīn-goō? Who am I?*

In this unit you will learn how to:
▶ *say what you do for a living.*
▶ *say how old you are.*
▶ *talk about your family.*
▶ *describe people.*
▶ *say numbers from 1 to 30.*

CEFR (A1): *Can ask for and provide personal information; can describe his/her family; can describe people; can handle numbers.*

🔘 香港人 Hèung-góng yàhn Hong Kongers

The English name Hong Kong is derived from two Chinese characters whose literal meaning is 'fragrant harbour', perhaps a reference to the fact that incense used to be made in factories along the coast there. It has long been one of the most densely populated cities in the world, and in recent decades, the population has soared to seven million.

Hong Kong people are known to be go-getters. They are efficient, hardworking, and, to a certain extent, resilient to change. Although there was a shift of Chinese to British sovereignty in 1841, and back to Chinese in 2007, the people have adapted with determination to both the Chinese and Western cultures. When space allows, Hong Kongers quite often live in an extended family. When you visit their homes, you may have a good chance of meeting not just their **taai-táai** (*wife*) or **sīn-sāang** (*husband*), but also their **sai-louh-jái** (*children*), father and mother, and maybe their **gūng-gūng** (*maternal grandpa*) and **pòh-pó** (*maternal grandma*), **yèh-yé** (*paternal grandpa*), and **màh-má** (*paternal grandma*). Like many other cultures, Hong Kongers are interested in visitors, and will casually ask **Néih jouh sīnhg-hòhng aa?** (*What do you do for a living?*); **Néih yáuh-móuh néuih/nàahm-páhng-yáuh aa?** (*Do you have a girlfriend/boyfriend?*); **Néih yáuh-móuh sai-louh-jái aa?** (*Do you have children?*). If you have, just say **Ngóh-yáuh** (*I have*), or otherwise, say **Ngóh móuh-aa** (*I don't*). Don't be intimidated by those questions, though. The more they want to be your **páhng-yáuh** (*friend*), the more intimate questions they will ask.

 How do you say *Do you have . . . ?* in Cantonese?

Vocabulary builder

02.01 Listen to the audio and match the Cantonese and the English. Then, listen again and try to imitate the speakers.

職業 *JĬK-YIHP* OCCUPATIONS

a	護士	wuh-sih	**1**	journalist
b	經理	gīng-léih	**2**	university student
c	記者	gei-jé	**3**	nurse
d	老師	lóuh-sī	**4**	manager
e	大學生	daaih hohk-sāang	**5**	teacher

生詞 *SĀANG-CHÌH* NEW EXPRESSIONS

有無?	yáuh-móuh	*have-have not*
做嘢?	jouh-yéh?	*work* (literally *what work?*)
做乜嘢?	jouh māt-yéh?	*What do you do?* (formal; literally *Do what?*)
我個仔	ngóh go-jái	*my son*
都係	dōu-haih	*is also*
咁	gám	*so*
好	hóu	*good*

年紀 *NÌHN-GÉI* AGE

幾大呀?	Géi-daaih aa?	*How old?* (literally *how big?*)
二十歲	yih-sahp seui	*twenty years old*
二十二歲	yih-sahp-yih seui	*twenty-two years old*

工作 *GŪNG-JOK* WORK

返工	fāan-gūng	*work* (literally *go to work*)
教書	gaau-syū	*teach*
讀緊書	duhk-gán syū	*studying*
讀歷史	duhk lihk-sí	*study history*
讀工程	duhk gūng-chìhng	*study engineering*

工作地點 *GŪNG-JOK DEIH-DÍM* WORK PLACES

醫院	yī-yún	*hospital*
銀行	ngàhn-hòhng	*bank*
中學	jūng-hohk	*secondary school*
南華早報	Nàahm-wàh-jóu-bou	South China Morning Post (*a prestigious Hong Kong newspaper*)

PARTICLES USED IN THIS UNIT

嘅	ge	Particle: making a statement more emphatic. When it follows **haih**, it asserts the intention.
喎	wo	Particle: expressing recognition with slight surprise.
添	tīm	Particle: meaning also, too, or as well.

 Conversation 1

02.02 *Listen to Sam-yi, Gaa-hou, and Pui-ling talking about what they do for a living.*

1 What is Sam-yi's job?

Gaa-hou	Aa-Yìh, jóu-sàhn!
Sam-yi	Aa-Hòuh, néih-hóu!
Gaa-hou	Aa-ìh, nèih yáuh-móuh jóuh-yéh aa?
Sam-yi	Yáuh-aa. Ngóh haih-go wuh-sih, hái yī-yún fāan-gūng.
Gaa-hou	Gám néih sīn-sàang jouh-māt aa?
Sam-yi	Kéuih hái ngàhn-hòhng fāan-gūng. Kéuih haih-go gīng-léih, néih nē?
Gaa-hou	Ngóh haih-go gei-jé, h Nàam-wàh-jóu-bou fāan-gūng.
Sam-yi	Gám néih taai-táai haih-m̀h-haih gei-jé aa?
Gaa-hou	Kéuih-m̀h-haih gei-jé. Kéuih-hái jūng-hohk gaau-syū.
	Sam-yi turns to Pui-ling.
Sam-yi	Aa-Lìhng, néih haih-m̀h-haih juhng duhk-gán syū nē?
Pui-ling	Haih aa, ngóh-hái daaih-hohk duhk-lihk-sí.
Sam-yi	Néih géi-dō-seui aa?
Pui-ling	Ngóh yih-sahp seui laa.
Sam-yi	Ngóh go-jái aa-Mìhng yih-sahp-yih seui, kéuih dōu-haih daaih-hohk-sāang, duhk gūng-chíhng.

2 What phrases from the dialogue mean the following?

   a Do you work?
   b What does your husband do?
   c He is a manager.
   d She is teaching in a secondary school.

3 Read Conversation 1 again and answer the questions.

   a What does Gaa-hou's wife do?
   b What is Pui-ling studying?
   c How old is she?
   d What is aa-Mìhng studying?

> **LANGUAGE TIP**
> As in English, you can shorten the phrase **Ngóh yih-sahp seui laa** simply to **yi-sap seui**. However, to avoid sounding abrupt or rude, it would be better to leave **laa** at the end of the sentence.

4 02.03 Listen to Conversation 1 line by line and repeat. Pay attention to the pronunciation.

Language discovery 1

1 **Which word from the conversation has been used for *is/am/are*, as in *I am a nurse, He is a bank manager*?**

2 **Which word from the conversation has been used for *a*, as in *I am a nurse, He is a bank manager*?**

3 **What is the Cantonese for *I'm twenty years old* in the conversation?**

係 *HAIH*

In a sense, Cantonese verbs are much simpler than English. They do not change for person or number. There are no different forms for different tenses. Look at the following sentences and note how the verb **haih** does not change as the verb does in English:

Ngóh haih-**go wu-si.**	*I **am** a nurse.*
Kéuih haih-**go ngàhn-hòhng gīng-léih.**	*He **is** a bank manager.*
Kéuih haih-**go gei-jé.**	*She **is** a journalist.*
Kéuih-dei haih **daaih-hohk-sāang.**	*They **are** university students.*

You might have gathered from the examples that the verb **haih** is the equivalent of *is/am/are* in Conversation 1. However, **haih** is not always used in ways that match English. In many cases, statements where English speakers would use the verb *be* are made without **haih** in Cantonese. You have already met examples in Unit 1, where *is/am/are* are simply replaced by two 'action' words **hóu** (*good*) and **sing** (*name/call*):

Néih hóu-**maa?**	*How **are** you?* (literally *you good* + **maa**)
Ngóh hóu-hóu.	*I **am** very well.* (literally *I good good*)
Néih gwai-sing **nē?**	*What **is** your name?* (literally *you what name* + **ne**)
Ngóh sing-**Léih.**	*I **am** Lee.* (literally *I call Lee*)

NEGATIVE FORMS

Go back to Conversation 1, and read it carefully. Which word indicates *not* (= negative form)?

To form the negative of **haih**, we put **m̀h** (*not*) in front of it, forming **m̀h-haih** (literally *not is/am/are*). For example:

Ngóh haih gō **wuh-sih.**	*I am a nurse.*
Ngóh m̀h-haih **gō wuh-sih.**	*I am not a nurse.*
Kéuih haih **go gei-je.**	*She is a journalist.*
Kéuih m̀h-haih **go gei-jé.**	*She is not a journalist.*

QUESTIONS

Read Conversation 1 again carefully. This time look for a sentence construction starting with **haih-m̀h-haih**. Is this a positive statement, a negative statement, or a question?

Interestingly, adding **haih** before **m̀h-haih** turns a statement into a question:

Néih haih-m̀h-haih Jūng-gwok-yàhn aa?
Are you Chinese? (literally *You be not be a Chinese person?* See Unit 1.)

Gám, néih tai-tái haih-m̀h-haih gei-jé aa?
So, is your wife a journalist? (literally *Your wife be not be a journalist?*)

個 GO

English uses *a* or *an* with words of occupation as in *I'm **a** nurse. He's **an** engineer*. In Cantonese, we use the word **go**, which belongs to a class of words that mark nouns with such similar features as shape or function. We call them **classifiers** (or **measures**). One of the most frequently used classifiers is **go**, which is not just for describing people, but also precedes such concrete things (very often 'roundish' in shape) as *apple* and *pear*, and abstract concepts such as *dream* and *suggestion*. However, in this unit, we will mainly use it for people and their occupations. Some examples are:

Ngóh go néuih-pàhng-yáuh haih-go lóuh-sī.	*My girlfriend is a teacher.*
Kéuih sīn-sāang haih-go yī-sāng.	*Her husband is a doctor.*
Néih tai-tái haih-go gei-jé?	*Your wife is a journalist?*
Kéuih haih-go ngàhn-hòhng gīng-léih.	*He is a bank manager.*

> **LANGUAGE TIP**
>
> **Sīn-sāang** has more than one meaning and can refer to *husband* or *teacher*. We use both in this unit.

Practice 1

1 Complete the sentences with *haih*, *m̀h-haih*, or *x* (nothing), as appropriate.

a Kéuih _____-go lóuh-sí.

b Néih-hóu, néih _____ jouh māt-yéh aa?

c Ngóh _____-go wuh-sih. Néih sīn-sāang jouh _____ māt-yéh aa?

d Ngo go-jái haih duhk lihk-síh, Kéuih _____ duhk gūng-cíng.

2 Put *go* in the correct place by inserting the symbol ^.

a Keuih nàahm-pàhng-yáuh haih yih-sāang.

b Ngóh gùhng-gūng haih lóuh-sī.

c Keuih jái yī-sahp-seui.

d Ngóh haih wuh-sih, haih yī-yún fāan-gūng.

3 Use what you know to answer these questions about yourself.

a Néih-giu mē-meng nē?   **c** Néih-jouh māt-yéh aa?

b Néih géi-do seui aa?   **d** Hái bīn-dōuh fāan-gūng?

Listen and understand

1 02.04 What do the following people do for a living? Listen and match the names with the jobs.

a	Sam-yi	**1**	ngàhn-hòhng gīng-lēih
b	Mr Lee	**2**	daaih-hohk-sāang
c	Mrs Wong	**3**	wuh-sih
d	Gaa-hou	**4**	lóuh-sī
e	Pui-ling	**5**	yī-sāang
f	Ah-ming	**6**	gei-jé

2 Read Conversation 1 again and underline the numbers 20 and 22. What do they look like?

3 Numbers in Cantonese are very straightforward. Try to complete the missing numbers before listening to the recording.

0	lìng	6	luhk	12	sahp-yih	18	sahp-____
1	yāt	7	chāt	13	____-sām	19	sahp-____
2	yih	8	baat	14	____-sei	20	yih-sahp
3	sāam	9	gáu	15	____-ńgh	21	yih-sahp-yāt (20+1)
4	sei	10	sahp	16	sahp-luhk	22	yih-sahp-____
5	ńgh	11	sahp-yāt (10+1)	17	sahp-____	30	sāam-sahp

4 02.05 **Now listen, repeat, and check whether you have got the missing numbers correct.**

5 02.06 **Now listen to some numbers in pairs. First write the number down. Then, listen again. This time, try to imitate the pronunciation of the speaker.**

a __1__ , __11__   f ____ , ____
b ____ , ____   g ____ , ____
c ____ , ____   h ____ , ____
d ____ , ____   i ____ , ____
e ____ , ____   j ____ , ____ , __30__

V More words!

02.07

家庭成員 *GĀ-TÍHNG SÍHNG-YÙHN* FAMILY MEMBERS

細路	sai-louh (short for sai-louh-jái)	*children*
仔, 女	jái, néui	*son, daughter*
兄弟姊妹	hīng-daih jí-muih	*brothers and sisters* (an umbrella term for kinship)
哥哥, 妹妹	gòh-gō, mùih-múi	*elder brother, younger sister*

形容詞 *YÌHNG-YUHNG-CHÌH* DESCRIPTIVE WORDS

後生	hauh-sāang	*young*
高, 瘦	gōu, sau	*tall, thin*
靚仔	leng-jái	*handsome* (literally *handsome boy*)

其他 *KÈIH-TĀ* OTHERS

幾個	Géi-gō?	*How many?*
幾大	Géi-daaih?	*How old?*
就係	jauh-haih	*that is*
同埋	tung-máaih	*and*
多謝	dō-jeh	*thank you* (for a service or a compliment)

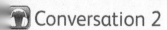 Conversation 2

02.08 *Listen as Sam-yi, Gaa-hou, and Pui-ling talk about their families.*

1 How many children does Gaa-hou have? What are their ages?

Sam-yi	Néih-yóuh géi-gō sai-louh-jái nē?
Gaa-hou	Ngóh-yáuh léuhng-go sai-louh. Yāt go-jái, yāt go-néui.
Sam-yi	Kéuih-deih gé-daaih aa?
Gaa-hou	Ngóh-go-jái sei-seui. Ngóh-go-néui léuhng-seui.
Sam-yi	Aa-Ling, néih yáuh géi-gō hīng-daih jí-muih aa?
Pui-ling	Ngóh yáuh yāt-go gòh-gō, yāt-go mùih-múi.
	Showing Sam-yi a photo . . .
	Kéuih-deih jauh-haih ngóh bàh-bā, màh-mā, tung-máaih gòh-gō laa.
Sam-yi	Néih bàh-bā, má-mā tái-lohk-heui hóu haauh-sāang wo. Néih aa-gō hóu-leng-jái tīm!
Pui-ling	Dō-jeh. Ngóh gòh-gō hóu-gōu.
	Aa-Pui, Sam-yi's daughter, is walking towards them. Pointing to Aa-Pui . . .
Sam-yi	Ngóh-go néui aa-Pui hóu-sau.

2 Read Conversation 2 carefully, then answer the questions.

    a How many brothers and sisters does Pui-ling have?
    b What does Pui-ling's brother look like?
    c What does Sam-yi's daughter look like?

> **LANGUAGE TIP**
>
> As already mentioned, numbers in Cantonese are straightforward. They are pronounced the same on all occasions, except the number 2 **yih**. When we count, we say **yāt**, **yih**, **sāam** . . . (1, 2, 3 . . .). However, when the numbers are followed by a classifier, 2 is pronounced **léuhng**, as in **léuhng gōu sai-louh** (*two children*) and **léuhng seui** (*two years old*).

💡 Language discovery 2

Go back to Conversation 2. This time try to locate the sentences indicating *I have two children* **and** *I have one older brother and one younger sister.*

有 YÁUH

If **haih** is the equivalent of *is/am/are*, then **yáuh** is similar to *have* in English. Like all Cantonese verbs, **yáuh** remains unchanged in all circumstances. But unlike **haih**, we cannot add **m̀h** (*not*) in front of it to form the negative. (It is wrong to say **m̀h-yáuh*.) We make the negative by changing **yáuh** into **móuh** (Note: **yáuh** is the only word in Chinese that doesn't go with **m̀h**.) For example, if you have a young sister, you could say **Ngóh-yáuh go mùih-múi**, and if you don't have one, then you should say **Ngóh-móuh mùi-múi**.

Another interesting point is when we put **yáuh** and **móuh** together, forming **yáuh-móuh**, a statement becomes a question.

ℹ️ Practice 2

1 Study the following example carefully, then fill in the blanks of the rest of the sentences. Read the questions and answers out loud.

Question	Yes	No
a Néih yáuh-móuh néuih-pàhng-yáuh aa?	Yáuh, ngóh-yáuh.	Móuh, ngóh-móuh.
Do you have a girlfriend?	*Yes, I have.*	*No, I haven't.*
b Néih _____ sai-louh-zái aa?	Yáuh, _____.	_____, ngóh móuh.
Do you have children?	*Yes, I have.*	*No, I haven't.*
c Néh yáuh-móuh nàahm-páhng-yáuh aa?	_____, ngóh yáuh.	Móuh, _____.
Do you have a boyfriend?	*Yes, I have.*	*No, I don't.*
d Néih yáuh-móuh jouh-yéh aa?	_____.	_____.
Are you working?	*Yes, I am.*	*No, I am not.*
literally *You have-have not work?*	literally *Yes, I have.*	literally *No, I have not.*

20

 Reading

It is safe to say that numbers are a significant part of Chinese culture. As the common saying goes, **hóuh-sih sìhng-sēung** (*good things come in pairs*). Even numbers are customarily regarded as more auspicious than odd ones. Pronunciation is another factor that determines whether a number is lucky or not. Six, eight, and nine are good numbers as their sounds are similar to words that have positive meanings. Here are some stories relating to numbers from zero to ten, and a glimpse into this vast subject.

1 **Guess what the following three characters represent, and write down their equivalents in English or in figures.**

一	**yāt**	____	Regarded as ominous; when used on its own, it implies loneliness.
二	**yih**	____	Regarded as lucky for it suggests germination and harmony.
三	**sām**	____	A good number indicating multiples, and the three stages of one's life – birth, marriage, and death.

2 **It would be useful to know the shape of numbers 4 to 10 too. Although they are a bit more complicated than 1–3, it may well be useful to be able to recognize them if you meet them.**

四	**sei**	*four*	The most unlucky number of all because it sounds like **séi** (*death*).
五	**ńgh**	*five*	Associates with *not*, and can be regarded as both negative as in **m̀h-faat** (*not prosperous*), and positive as in **m̀h-séi** (*no death*).
六	**luhk**	*six*	Auspicious in general, but in Cantonese it resembles the sound **lohk** (*fall*).
七	**chāt**	*seven*	A good number when it symbolizes *togetherness* but **chāt-yuht** (*July*) is said to be a ghost month – a month in which ghosts and spirits are said to return to the land of the living.
八	**baat**	*eight*	Famous for its auspiciousness because it sounds like **faat** (*prosperous*).
九	**gáu**	*nine*	Sounds the same as **gáu** (*long-lasting*), and is said to be associated with emperors of China.
十	**sahp**	*ten*	Denotes completeness as in **sahp-cyùhn sahp-máih** (*perfect*).

3 **Knowing what zero looks like is also important:**

| 零 | **lìng** | *zero* | Not auspicious, implying *emptiness* **lìhng-dīng** and *loneliness* as in **gūlìhng**. |

📝 Writing

The basic rule for writing Chinese characters is from top to bottom and from left to right. Nowadays we can write Chinese on a page the same way we write English, that is from left to right. The ancient way of writing Chinese is from top to bottom. At present, there are still books published in such a style.

There are eight basic strokes:

1 **dot**

2 **horizontal stroke**

3 **turning stroke and vertical stroke**

4 **hook stroke**

5 **right-upward stroke**

6 **left-downward stroke**

7 **short right-upward stroke**

8 **right-downward stroke.**

All can be found in a single character 永 **wínhg** (*forever*):

Interpretations vary, but the basic concepts are more or less the same. For fun, why not try to imitate this word to get a taste of Chinese writing!

1 Complete the following sentences by filling in the blanks.

   a Néih _____ jouh-yéh aa?

   b Ngóh _____ dáaih-hohk duhk syū.

   c Kéuih _____ néuih-pànhg-yáuh _____ wuh-sih.

   d Ngóh haih ngàhn-hòhng gīng-léih. Néih j _____?

   e Néih sīn-sāang j _____ aa? or Néih sīn-sāang j _____ aa?

   f Néih _____ Jūng-gwōk-yàhn aa?

2 02.09 Listen to Suk-yi introducing herself and her family, then answer the questions.

Ngóh-giu aa-yì, yih-sahp-baat seui. Ngóh-haih-go lóuh-sī. Ngóh-gō-jái baat-seui; ngóh-gō-néui sahp-yāt seui.

   a How old is Suk-yi?

   b How old are her children?

   c What does she do?

SELF CHECK

	I CAN . . .
○	. . . say what I do for a living.
○	. . . say how old I am.
○	. . . talk about my family.
○	. . . describe people.
○	. . . say numbers from 1 to 30.

3 行街買嘢
Haang-gaai Maai-ye
Go shopping

In this unit you will learn to:
▶ *find out how much things cost.*
▶ *shop for clothes by size and colour.*
▶ *say numbers from 30 to 1,000,000,000.*

CEFR (A1): *Can make simple purchases by stating what is wanted and asking the price; can handle numbers; can ask for clarification.*

 購物舒緩療法
Kau-maht syū-wùhn lìuh-faat *Retail therapy*

Hong Kong is a shopping paradise, where you can pick up almost everything at a reasonable price, from **sihk-maht** (*food*) to **yī-fuhk** (*clothes*) to **gūng-ngaih-bán** (*handicrafts*). Like any other big city, Hong Kong has both **chīu-kăp síh-chèuhng** (*supermarkets*) and **sēung-chèuhng** (*shopping malls*). But what makes shopping in Hong Kong so agreeable are the traditional **gāai-síh** (*wet markets*), the **gāai-bīn-dong** (*street stalls*), and especially **daaih-pàih-dong** (*open food stalls*) in such places as Stanley, the alleys in Central, and the ladies' market in Mongkok, where **góng-ga** (*bargaining*) is common. Particularly smart shoppers equip themselves with phrases like **Géi-dō-chín-aa?** (*How much is it?*), **Taai-gwai laa!** (*Too expensive!*), and **Néih hó-m̀h-hó-yíh gáam-ga aa?** (*Could you reduce the price?*).

The word for *money* is **chín**. **Góng-jí** (*Hong Kong dollars*) is the local currency, but these days **yàhn-màhn-baih** (*Riminbi, the currency of the People's Republic of China*) is also used.

 What is the Cantonese for *money*? What is the currency used in Hong Kong, and what is the currency used in the People's Republic of China?

> **LANGUAGE TIP**
> **Góng-jí** literally means *Hong Kong paper*. The formal name for the *Hong Kong dollar* is **góng-baih**. **Baih** on its own means *currency*.

Vocabulary builder

Complete the missing English expressions, then listen to the audio and try to imitate the pronunciation of the speakers.

衣服 *YĪ-FUHK* CLOTHING

鞋	hàaih	*shoe*
衫	sāam (short for sēut-sāam)	*shirt (informal)*
裙, 褲	kwàhn, fu	*dress/skirt, trousers*
T-恤	tī-sēut	*T-shirt*
外套	ngoih-tou	*jacket*
冷衫	lāang-sāam	*sweater*
女裝恤衫	néuih-jōng sēut-sāam	*blouse for _____*
男裝恤衫	nàahm-jōng sēut-sāam	*_____ for men*

> **LANGUAGE TIP**
>
> 03.02 A faster and more fun way to remember the colours in question is to memorize this rhyme: **hūng, wòhng, làahm, baahk, hāk, ga-fēi lōu cháang-jāp**. (literally *red, yellow, blue, white, black, coffee mixed with orange juice*)

顏色 *NGÀAHN-SĪK* COLOUR

紅, 黃, 藍	hùhng, wòhng, làahm	*red, yellow, blue*
白, 黑	baahk, hāk	*white, black*
咖啡	ga-fēi	*brown*
橙, 灰, 綠	cháang, fūi, luhk	*orange, grey, green*

03.02 生詞 *SĀANG-CHÌH* NEW EXPRESSIONS

提問 *Tàih-mahn* Question words

有無?	Yáuh-móuh?	*Do you have?*
幾多錢呢?	Géi-dō chín nē?	*How much?*
你想要?	Néih séung-yiu?	*What do you want?*
咩顏色呢?	Mē ngàan-sīk nē?	*What colour?*
可唔可以?	Hó-m̀h-hó yi?	*Can I?*
啱唔啱身呀?	Ngāam-m̀h-ngāam sān aa?	*Does it fit?*
大咗啲?	daaih-jóu dī?	*A bit bigger?*
細一碼?	sai yāt-máh?	*A smaller size?*
你重想要啲咩呢?	Néih juhng-séung yiu dī mē nē?	*What else do you want?*

其他 *Kèih-tā* Other expressions

又	yauh	*also*
啱	ngāam	*fit (literally correct)*
呢件	nī-gihn	*this*
嗰件	gó-gihn	*that*
定係	dihng-haih	*or*
著緊	jeuk-gán	*wearing*
試身, 試身室	si-sān, si-sān-sāt	*try it on, fitting room*
啱晒你	ngāam-saai néih	*fits you well (literally fit well you)*
我買咗佢喇	Ngóh máaih-jó keuih lāa!	*I'll take it!*

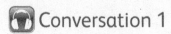
Conversation 1

03.03 *This is the first time Mary and her colleague John have visited Hong Kong. Mary goes into a shop on Festival Walk to buy some clothes and talks to the sauh-fo-yùhn (sales assistant).*

1 What does Mary want to buy?

Mary	Chíng-mahn nī-gihn-sāam géi-dō chín nē?
Sauh-fo-yùhn	Yí-baak-cāt-sahp mān.
Mary	Néih yáuh-móuh sāam-sahp-baat máh aa?
Sauh-fo-yùhn	Yáuh, néih yiu-mē ngàahn-sīk nē? Baahk-sīk? Hùhng-sīk? Dihng-haih nàahm-sīk nē?
Mary	Baahk-sīk lāa.
Sauh-fo-yùhn	Hóu-aa, nī-gihn-haih baahk-sīk.
Mary	Ngóh hó-m̀h-hó-yíh si-háh kéuih aa?
Sauh-fo-yùhn	Hó-yíh, si-sān-sāt hái gó-bihn. *(Later)* Ngāam-m̀h-ngāam sān aa?
Mary	Daaih-jóu dī, yáuh-móuh sai-yāt-máh nē?
Sauh-fo-yùhn	Yáuh, nī-gihn haih sāam-sahp-luhk máh.
Mary	Nī-gihn hóu ngāam-sān. Ngóh máaih-jó keuih lāa!
Sauh-fo-yùhn	Haih-aa, ngāam-saai néih aa. Néih juhng-séung yiu-dī-mē nē?
Mary	Néih yáuh-móuh hāk-sīk-ge chèuhng-fu aa? *(pointing at the trousers)* Kéuih-deih yauh gei-dō-chín aa?

2 Read the conversation and answer the questions.

   a What colours does the blouse come in?

   b Does the first blouse that Mary tries on fit her?

   c What else does she want to buy?

> **LANGUAGE TIP**
> Note the tone: **hái** (*in/at*) and **haih** (*is/am/are*)

3 Match the questions and answers.

   a Néih yiu-mē ngàahn-sīk nē?

   b Ngóh hó-m̀h-hó-yíh si-sān aa?

   c Ngāam-m̀h-ngāam-sān aa?

   d Yáuh-móuh sai-yát-máh nē?

   e Néih juhng-séung-yiu-di mē nē?

   1 Nī-gihn sai-dī, sāam-sahp-luhk máh.

   2 Néih yáuh-móuh chèuhng-fu aa?

   3 Baahk-sīk lāa.

   4 Hóu ngāam-sān.

   5 Hó-yíh, si-sān-sāt hai gó-bihn.

🔎 Language discovery

Find the following two expressions in Conversation 1. What do they mean? Can you find the word indicating *no/not*?

a hó-m̀h-hó-yíh

b ngāam m̀h-ngāam-sān

Putting **m̀h** in front of a verb turns it into a negative form. So, **hó-yíh** means *can* and **mh-hó-yíh** means *cannot*. **Ngáam-sán** means *fit well* in the dialogue, and **m̀h-ngāam-sān** means *don't fit well*.

QUESTION FORMS

唔 . . . M̀H . . . NOT . . .

Hó-m̀h-hó-yíh literally means *can-not-can*, and **ngāam-m̀h-ngāam-sān** literally means *fit-not-fit*.

If you have worked through Units 1 and 2, you will have met the expression **haih-m̀h-haih**. Is there any similarity between this structure and those in **hó-m̀h-hó-yíh** and **ngāam-m̀h-ngāam-sān**?

Yes, by putting the positive and the negative forms side by side, a statement becomes a question, as in:

Néih haih m̀h-haih Jŭng-gwok-yàhn aa?	*Are you Chinese?*
Ngóh hó-m̀h-hó-yíh si-san aa?	literally *Can I try it on?*
Ngāam-m̀h-ngāam-sān aa?	*Does it fit?*

03.04 **If a verb contains two words, as in hó-yíh (*can*) and ngāam-sān (*fit-well*), to create a question we can simply keep the first word of each expression to mark the positive, followed by the negative. So the questions will start with hó m̀h-hó-yíh . . . ? and ngāam m̀h-ngāam-sān . . . ?**

At the end of such expressions as **hó-m̀h-hó-yi . . . ?** and **ngāam-m̀h-ngāam-sān . . . ?**, Cantonese speakers will normally add the particle **aa** to make it really clear that it is a question. Alternatively, we can of course simply raise the tone of the closing word (much as we do in English):

Néih haih-m̀h-haih Jūng-gwok-yàhn aa? or
Nei haih-m̀h-haih Jūng-gwok-yàhn? (raise the tone of **yàhn**, making
the sound **yán**)

Ngo hó-m̀h-hó-yi si-sān aa? or
Ngo hó-m̀h-hó-yi si-sān? (raise the tone of **sān**)

Ngāam-m̀h-ngāam-sān aa? or
Ngāam m̀h-ngāam-sān? (raise the tone of **sān**)

幾 *GEI* HOW

Go back to Conversation 1, and find a sentence with the word **gei**. How
close does it look to the question **Néih géi-daaih aa?** (see Unit 2)?

Géi is similar to the English question word *how*. So,

Néih géi-daai aa?	*How old are you?*
Kéuih géi-dō-cín aa?	*How much is it?*

Don't forget these useful descriptive words: **gōu** (*tall*), **ngái** (*short*), **fèih**
(*fat*), **sau** (*thin*), **daaih** (*big*) and **sai** (*small*).

有無 *YÁUH-MÓUH* HAVE/HAVE NOT AND *HAIH VH-HAIH* BE/BE NOT

We looked at the two-word expression **yáuh-móuh** (*have/have not*) in
Unit 2. Can you see the similarity of the phrase structures **yáuh-móuh**
and **haih-m̀h-haih** (*be/be not*)?

These two expressions operate on the same principle. By putting together
the positive and negative forms of a verb, a statement is now turned into
a question, as with:

Néih *haih-m̀h-haih* Jūng-gwok-yàhn aa?	*Are you Chinese?*
Néih *yáuh-móuh* sāam-sahp-bāat máh aa?	*Do you have size 38?*
Néih *yáuh-móuh* chín aa?	*Do you have money?*
Néih *yáuh-móuh* sai-gihn dī aa?	*Do you have a smaller one?*

CLASSIFIERS

In Unit 2, we learned one of the most frequently used classifiers, **go**, which is used to talk about a number of objects. However, the most frequently used classifier for clothing is **gihn**, followed by **tìuh** and **deui**, as follows:

Gihn for most clothing:

yāt-gihn sāam	*one shirt*
léuhng-gihn tēe-sēut	*two T-shirts*
sāam-gihn ngoih-tou	*three jackets*

> **LANGUAGE TIP**
> **Sāam** (*shirt*) is short for **sēut-sāam**, which is a more formal usage.

Tìuh is used for such 'longish' clothing as skirts, dresses, and trousers:

ńgh-tìuh kwàhn	*five skirts/dresses*
luhk-tìuh fu	*six pairs of trousers*

Deui is used for most kinds of clothing that come in pairs, as with:

gáu-deui hàaih	*nine pairs of shoes*
sahp-deui ngáahn-géng	*ten pairs of glasses*

> **LANGUAGE TIP**
> Note that the classifier for trousers is **tìuh**, as in **yāt-tìuh fu** (*a pair of trousers*). It might well be that the 'length' of the trousers appeared more significant than the notion of 'pair' when the expression was first used.

呢個 *NĪ-GO* **THIS**, 嗰個 *GÓ-GO* **THAT**, 呢啲 *NĪ-DĪ* **THESE**, 嗰啲 *GÓ-DĪ* **THOSE**

To make your shopping experience more effective in Cantonese, learn to say the equivalents of **nī-go** *this* and **gó-go** *that*, **nī-dī** *these* and **gó-dī** *those*. In English, you would be understood if you just said *this skirt* and *that shirt*, but in Cantonese we need to include the appropriate classifiers to complete such expressions, as in:

nī-gihn saam	*this shirt*
ngàahn-géng	*that pair of glasses*
nī-tìuh kwàhn	*this skirt*
gó-go yàhn	*that person*
nī-dī fu	*these trousers*
gó-dī lāang-sāam	*those sweaters*

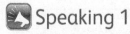 **Practice**

1 **Give the Cantonese equivalents for the following questions.**
   a How big is it?
   b How tall/short are you?
   c How small is it?
   d How fat/thin are you?

2 **Translate the following into English, and then say the words in Cantonese.**
   a Gáu-gihn néuih-jōng sēut-sāam
   b Sāam-tìuh fu
   c Yāt-deui ngáahn-géng

3 **Translate the following into English, then say the lines in Cantonese.**
   a Ngóh hó-m̀h-hó-yíh si-háh nī-gihn fuī-sī sēut-sāam aa? *May I try . . .*
   b Ngóh hó-m̀h-hó-yíh si-háh gó-gihn wòhng-sīk láan-sāam aa?
   c Ngóh hó-m̀h-hó-yíh si-háh nī-tìuh hung-sīk-fu aa?
   d Ngóh hó-m̀h-hó-yíh si-háh gó-tìuh cháang-sīk-kwàhn aa?

Speaking 1

You are standing in front of a street stall in Stanley and spot a shirt that you like. Try to say the following out loud in Cantonese.

a How much does that shirt cost?
b Do you have a green one?
c Do you have size 32?
d May I try that skirt on?

Listen and understand

CHINESE NUMBERS
Numbers 1 to 100

Chinese numbers are based on a decimal system. Numbers 0–9 can be represented by both Chinese characters and Arabic numerals. The system is straightforward and logical:

10 is **sahp** (*ten*); 20 is **yih-sahp** (*two-ten*); 30 is **sāam-sahp** (*three-ten*); and so on up to 90.

11 is **sahp-yāt** (*ten-one*); 12 is **sahp-yih** (*ten-two*); and so on up to 19.

21 is **yih-sahp-yāt** (*two-ten-one*); 34 is **sāam-sahp-sei** (*three-ten-four*).

45 is **sei-sahp-ńgh** (*four-ten-five*); and so on up to 99 **gáu-sahp-gáu** (*nine-ten-nine*).

 1 03.05 **Try to complete the numbers before listening to the audio. Then listen to check your answers. Finally, listen again and try to imitate the speakers and their pronunciation.**

Numbers 31 to 99

40	sei-sahp	31	sāam-sahp-_____
50	ńgh-sahp	32	sāam-_____
60	luhk-sahp	43	sei-sahp-_____
70	chāt-sahp	44	_____-sei
80	bāat-sahp	55	_____-ńgh
90	gáu-sahp	56	ńgh-sahp-_____
67	_____-cāt	84	baat-sahp _____
68	_____-baat	85	_____
69	luhk-sahp-_____	86	_____
71	_____-yāt	97	_____
72	chāt-_____	98	_____
73	_____	99	gáu-sahp-gáu

2 03.06 **Now follow the audio and practise counting from 1 to 99 before going further.**

Numbers 100 to 999

Baak is the Cantonese for *hundred*. So, 100 is **yāt-baak**; 200 is **yih-baak**, and so on up to 999 **gáu-baak gáu-sahp-gáu**. However, for numbers 101 to 109, we will also need to mention the zero involved, making 101(100-0-1) **yāt-baak lìhng-yāt**, 102 (100-0-2) **yāt-baak lìhng-yih**, and so on up to 109 (100-0-9) **yāt-baak lìhng-gáu**.

3 03.07 **Try to complete the blanks before listening to the audio. Then listen to check your answers. Finally, listen again and try to imitate the speakers and their pronunciation.**

100	yāt-baak	345	_____ sei-sahp-ngh
103	yāt-baak lìhng-_____	430	sei-baak _____
120	_____ yih-sahp	562	ngh-baak _____
200	yih-_____	670	_____ chāt-sahp
204	yih-bāak _____-sei	710	_____
261	_____-luhk-sahp-yāt	890	_____
300	sāam-_____	998	gáu-baak gáu-sahp-baat

Higher numbers

Chīn is the Cantonese for *thousand*. **Maahn** is *ten thousand* (10,000). So, **sahp-maahn** is *a hundred thousand* (100,000; in other words *ten ten-thousand*), and **baak-maahn** is *a million* (1,000,000; in other words *a hundred ten-thousand*). The most interesting and difficult number is the British *billion* (1,000,000,000), which is literally *ten billion* **sahp-yīk** in Cantonese (because **yīk** in Chinese is *a hundred million*, i.e. 100,000,000). Here is what these numbers look like:

1	yāt	
10	(yāt) sahp	**sahp** *is more frequently used than* **yāt-sahp**
100	(yāt-)baak	
1,000	(yāt-)chīn	
10,000	(yāt-)maahn	
100,000	(yāt) sahp-maahn	**sahp-maahn** *is always used without* **yāt**
1,000,000	(yāt-)baak-maahn	
1,000,000,000	(sahp-)yīk	**yāt-yīk** *is a hundred million in Chinese*

32

4 03.08 **Listen and fill in the prices of the following clothing.**

  a Nī-gihn sāam haih _____ mán.   **e** Nī-gihn lāang-sāam haih
  b Gó-tìuh kwàhn haih _____ mán.   _____ mán.
  c Nī-deui hàaih haih _____ mán.   **f** Gó-gihn ngoih-tou haih
  d Gó-tìuh fu haih _____ mán.   _____ mán.

5 03.09 **Peter is trying on some clothing. Listen and complete the sentences with what you hear.**

  a Nī-gihn lāan-sāam _____.   Chíng-mahn yáuh-móuh _____ nē?
  b Gó-tìuh kwàhn _____.   Chíng-mahn yáuh-móuh _____ nē?
  c Nī-deui hàaih _____.   Chíng-mahn yáuh-móuh _____ nē?
  d Gó-tìuh fu _____.   Chíng-mahn yáuh-móuh _____ nē?

Speaking 2

1 **Play the part of the customer in this conversation. The last one has been done for you.**

> **You** *Excuse me, how much are those shoes?*
> **Sauh-fo-yùhn** Yāt-bak baat-sahp-baat mān.
> **You** *Very expensive. Could you reduce the price?*
> **Sauh-fo-yùhn** Yat-bak baat-sap man laa.
> **You** Gáam aa. Ngóh máaih-jó-kéuih laa.
>   *(Is that so? I'll take them).*

2 **How do you say** *I'll take them* **in the conversation above?**

03.10 **Máaih** literally means *buy*, but note that it has a different tone from the very similar word **maaih**, which means *sell*! These two tones are quite close to each other. To avoid being misunderstood, practise – practice makes perfect!

3 **Read the following sentences out loud.**

  a Ngóh máaih-jó tìuh kwàhn.   *I've bought a skirt.*
  b Ngóh maaih-jó ngóh-ginh   *I've sold my sweater.*
       lāan-sāam.
  c Kéuih máaih-jó gó-gihn sūet-sāam. *He has bought that shirt.*
  d Kéuih maaih-jó gó-deui-hàaih.   *He has sold that pair of shoes.*
  e Néih máaih-jó tìuh-fu.   *You have bought a pair of trousers.*
  f Néih maaih-jó néih-gihn tī-sēut.   *You have sold your T-shirt.*

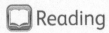

Reading

1 Can you figure out the missing percentages? Can you see the pattern?

折扣 *JIT-KAU* **DISCOUNTS**

九折	**gáu-jit**	*10 % off*	四折	**sei-jit**	___ *off*
八折	**baat-jit**	*20 % off*	三折	**sāam-jit**	*70 % off*
七折	**chāt-jit**	___ *off*	兩折	**léuhng-jit**	___ *off*
六折	**luhk-jit**	*40 % off*	一折	**yāt-jit**	*90 % off*
五折	**ńgh-jit**	*50 % off*			

Jit (*discounts*) is short for **jit-kau**. To indicate what the reduction is in English, we say *10 % off*, but in Cantonese we have to say **gáu-jit** (*90 % of the original price*). So if *a pair of trousers* has *40 % off* in English, in Cantonese it becomes **tìuh-fu luhk-jit**. Isn't it challenging?

2 **Now answer these questions.**
   a What items carry a 40 per cent discount?
   b What discount can you get for men's trousers?
   c What could you buy at a 30 per cent discount?

 # Test yourself

1 **Say the following in Cantonese.**
   a How much are those trousers? The blue ones.
   b I want size 46.
   c May I try them on?
   d A bit too small for me.
   e This shirt fits well.

2 03.11 **Listen and make a note of the clothes Mary and John are taking on their trip to Hong Kong.**

Mary: _____.

John: _____.

3 03.12 **Put the correct Cantonese beside the numbers before listening to the audio to check your answers.**

sāam-baak-baat-sahp-gáu	ngh-baak-gáu-saph
yih-baak-chāt-sahp-yāt	sahp-maahn
yih-chīn-ngh-baak	yāt-baak-sei-sahp-yi
chāt-baak luhk-sahp-chāt	

a 142   **e** 767
b 271   **f** 2,500
c 389   **g** 100,000
d 590

SELF CHECK

I CAN ...
○ ... find out how much things cost.
○ ... shop for clothes by size and colour.
○ ... say numbers from 30 to 1,000,000,000.

1 **At a party, Siu-ming meets Syu-kei. Complete the conversation with Néih (*you*) and Ngóh (*I*).**

Siu-ming	_____-hóu.
Syu-kei	_____-hóu, jóu-sàhn!
Siu-ming	_____-sing-Léih, chíng-máhn gwai-sing?
Syu-kei	_____-sing Chàhn.
Siu-ming	Chàhn síu-jé, _____ hóu-maa?
Syu-kei	_____ hóu-hóu! _____ nē, Léih sīn-sāang?
Siu-ming	_____ dōu géi-hóu ăa, dō-jeh.

Points: _____ /8

2 **Respond to the following:**
  a Hello!
  b Jóu-sàhn!
  c Ngóh-sing-Léih, gwai-sing nē?
  d Neíh-hóu-maa?
  e Ngóh hóu-hóu! Néih nē?

Points: _____ /5

3 R1.01 **Listen and complete the sentences with the missing words.**
  sīn-sāang   taai-táai   síu-jé   néuih-sih
  a Ngóh-hóu-hóu, Lèuhng _____.
  b Nèih-hóu-maa, Chēung _____?
  c Ngóh dōu-géi-hóu ăa, Nģh _____.
  d Wòhng _____, néih-hóu.

Points: _____ /4

4 R1.02 **Listen and choose the correct age for each person.**
  a Aa-ming 17/19   c Mr Lee 48/58   e gung-gung 73/63
  b Pui-ling 25/13   d po-po 58/61   f Gaa-hou 14/6

Points: _____ /6

5 **Give appropriate answers to the following questions.**
  a Which Cantonese word is used for *is/am/are* as in *I am a nurse*, *He is a bank manager*, and *They are students*?
  b Which Cantonese word is used for *a*, as in *I am a nurse* and *He is a bank manager*?
  c What is the Cantonese for *I'm twenty years old*.

Points: _____ /3

6 Turn the following statements into a) negative statements and b) questions.

Ngóh haih gō wuh-sih.

a _____

b _____

Kéuih-haih go gei-jé.

c _____

d _____

Néih haih Jŭng-gwok-yàhn.

e _____

f _____

Points: _____ /6

7 Complete the following phrases with a correct classifier.

a Yāt _____ saam.

b Ńgh _____ kwan.

c Gáu _____ haai.

Points: _____ /3

8 Read the following sentences carefully, and fill in the missing words.

a _____ fu   *these trousers*

b _____ yàhn   *that person*

c _____ kwàhn   *this skirt*

d _____ ngáahn-géng   *that pair of glasses*

Points: _____ /4

9 While shopping for clothes you see a blouse you like. How would you say the following in Cantonese?

a How much is that blouse?

b Do you have size 38?

c May I try it on?

d That one fits you very well.

e Do you have a smaller size?

f I want a white one.

Points: _____ /6

Total points: _____ /45

去邊喥 *Heui bīn-douh*

Where to go?

In this unit you will learn how to:

▶ *get travel information.*
▶ *confirm travel schedules.*
▶ *say the days of the week.*
▶ *ask and tell the time.*

CEFR (A1): *Can get simple information about travel using public transport; can indicate time.*

香港中國游 Hēung-góng Jūng-gwok yàuh *Getting by in Hong Kong and the Chinese mainland*

When you arrive at Hong Kong's Chek-lap-gok **fēi-gēi-chèuhng** (*airport*), the best way of getting to your hotel hassle-free is to hire a taxi. It costs about HK$250 from the airport to **Tsim-sha-tsui**, the **máah-tàuh** (*fragrant harbour*).

If you prefer a hi-tech experience, the **gēi-chèuhng faai-sin** (*Airport Express*) and the **MTR** (*Mass Transit Railway*) may serve you better. Or, to be economical, you could take a bus or **síu-bā** (*public minibus*) to many destinations, including going through the **hói-déi seuih-douh** (*Cross Harbour Tunnel*) to the waterside Convention and Exhibition Centre in Wan-Chai on Hong Kong Island.

Taking the **síu-lèuhn** (*ferry*) is a dramatic way of seeing the views along the harbour. If you want to go to **sāan-díng** (*Victoria Peak*) on the island, getting on a peak tram offers a magnificent view of the territory. Alternatively, you can go east on the island by taking a tram to Aberdeen, where you can have a delicious seafood dinner.

It is also worth visiting Macau and its casinos, and a turbojet will get you there in less than an hour. You can also take KCR trains to visit the nearby cities of Shenzhen and Guangzhau. But, if **maahn-léih chèuhng-sìhng** (the *Great Wall*, literally *ten-thousand-long-city*) near Beijing is your target, planes are plentiful.

Douh-hói síu-lèuhn literally means *cross-sea ferry*. Can you find its more commonly used short form in the text?

Vocabulary builder

04.01 **Complete the missing English expressions, then listen to the audio and try to imitate the pronunciation of the speakers.**

時間 *SÌH-GAAN* THE TIME

點, 點鐘	dím, dím-jūng	*time (literally dot/dot-clock)*
而家	yìh-gā	*now*
幾多點呀?	Géi-dō dím?	*What time is it?*
幾點呢?	Géi-dím nē?	*At what time?*
一點鐘	yāt-dím jūng	*one o'clock*
十二點三	sahp-yih dím-sāam	*quarter past _____*
七點半	chāt-dím bun	*half past _____*
三點九	sāam-dím gāu	*quarter to four*
五點四	ńgh-dím sei	*twenty past _____*
六點二	luhk-dím yih	*ten past _____*

交通公具 *GĀAU-TŪNG GŪNG-GEUIH* TRANSPORT

的士, 巴士	dīk-sí, bā-sí	*taxi, bus*
纜車, 山頂纜車	laahm-chē (short for sān-dīng laahm-chē)	*tram, peak tram*
地鐵, 地下鐵	deih-tit (short for deih-hah-tit)	*Mass Transit Railway (MTR)*
電車, 火車	dihn-chē, fó-chē	*tram, train*
噴射飛船	pan-seh fēi-syùhn	*turbojet*
搭	daap	*take*
搭飛機	daap fēi-gēi	*taking the plane*
搭機場快線	daap gēi-chèuhng faai-sin	*taking the Airport Express*
站	jaahm	*station*
巴士站	bā-sí jaahm	*bus station*

星期 *SĪNG-KÈIH* DAYS OF THE WEEK

星期日	Sīng-kèih yaht (note the tone)	*Sunday*
星期一	Sīng-kèih yāt (note the tone)	_____*day*
星期二	Sīng-kèih yih	_____
星期三	Sīng-kèih sāam	*Wednesday*
星期四	Sīng-kèih sei	_____
星期五	Sīng-kèih nǵh	*Friday*
星期六	Sīng-kèih luhk	_____

 Can you match numbers 1–6 that we looked at in Unit 2 with the Chinese characters representing the days of the week? Which expression represents Sunday?

生詞 *SĀANG-CHÌH* NEW EXPRESSIONS

唔該你	M̀h-gōi néih.	*Excuse me.*
我想買	Ngóh séung máaih . . .	*I would like to buy . . .*
火車飛	fó-chē fēi	*train tickets*
去廣州	heui Gwóng-jāu	*to Guangzhau*
邊日呢?	Bīn-yah nē?	*Which day?*
上晝	seuhng-jau	*morning*
定係	dihng-haih	*or*
下晝	hah-jau	*afternoon*
最早嗰班	Jeui jóu gó-bāan . . .	*When is the first . . .*
幾點?	Géi-dím?	*What time?*
到	dou	*arrives*
下一班	hah-yāt-bāan	*next (train, plane, etc.)*
上一班	seuhng-yāt-bāan	*last (train, plane, etc.)*
單程飛, 來回飛	dāan-chìhng fēi, lòih-wùih fēi	*single ticket, return ticket*
咁, 咁呀	gám, gám-aa	*Is that so?*

CLASSIFIERS USED IN THIS UNIT

張	jēung, as in yāt-jēung fēi	*a ticket*
班	bāan, as in hah-yāt-bāan fó-chē	*next train*
個	go, as in léuhng-go-jih	*ten minutes*

Conversation 1

04.02 *Joseph is buying a train ticket to Guangzhau. He talks to the sauh-piu yùhn (person at the ticket office) at Hunghom train station.*

1 What day does Joseph want to travel and at what time?

Joseph	M̀h-gōi néih, ngóh-séung máaih yāt-jēung heui Gwóng-jāu ge fó-chē fēi.
Sauh-piu yùhn	Bīn-yaht nē?
Joseph	Sahp-ńgh houh, Sīng-kéih yih.
Sauh-piu yùhn	Seuhng-jau dihng-hahi hah-jau nē?
Joseph	Seuhng-jau laa. Jeui jóu gó-bāan (fó-chē) haih gēi-dím aa?
Sauh-piu yùhn	Seuhng-jau chāt-dím bun yáuh yāt-bāan. Hah-yāt-bāan hái sahp-yih dím-sāam.
Joseph	Gám ngóh-yiu chāt-dím-bun gó-bāan laa. Gēi-dím dou Gwóng-jāu nē?
Sauh-piu yùhn	Hah-jau sāam-dím.
Joseph	Géi-chín nē?
Sauh-piu yùhn	Dāan-chìhng dihng-haih lòih-wùih nē?
Joseph	Dāan-chìhng laa.
Sauh-piu yùhn	Gám-aa, yāt-baak gáu-sahp mān Góng-jí laa.

More words!

Géi-dím? is short for **Géi-dō-dim?**	*What time?*
Géi-chín? is short for **Gei-dō-chín?**	*How much?*

2 Match the Cantonese and the English.

a	Bīn-yaht nē?	1 I would like to buy a train ticket.
b	Gēi-dō-dím dou?	2 Which day?
c	Dāan-chìhng dihng-haih lóih-wùih?	3 Morning or afternoon?
d	Gēi-chín nē?	4 When will it arrive?
e	Seuhng-jau dihng-haih hah-jau nē?	5 How much?
f	Ngóh séung máaih-jēung fó-chē fēi.	6 Single or return?

3 Read the conversation and answer the questions in English first, then answer them in Cantonese.

a On which day does Joseph want to travel?

b At what time of day?

c What time does the first train leave?

d What time does it arrive in Guangzhau?

e How much is it for a single (ticket)?

4 04.03 **Now listen to Conversation 1 line by line and repeat. Pay attention to the pronunciation.**

💡 Language discovery 1

1 **Find and underline the expressions in the dialogue which mean the following:**
   a at what time . . . ?
   b at half past seven
   c at a quarter past twelve

2 **To ask about arrival and departure times, Cantonese uses the expressions:**

   Géi-dō dím dou?   *When will it arrive?*

   Géi-dō dím hōi/jáu?   *When will it leave?*

> **LANGUAGE TIP**
> **hōi** (*drive away*; literally *open*); **jáu** (*leave*; literally *go*)

To reply to these questions, Cantonese people simply state the time. Look at the following extract from Conversation 1.

Joseph	Jeui-jóu gó-bāan haih gēi-dím aa?	*When is the earliest train?*
Sauh-piu yùhn	Seuhng-jau chāt-dím-bun.	*Seven o'clock in the morning.*
Joseph	Gēi-dō-dím dóu Gwóng-jāu nē?	*When will it arrive in Guangzhau?*
Sauh-piu yùhn	Hah-jau sāam-dím.	*Three o'clock in the afternoon.*

By now, you should have got that *three o'clock* is **sāam-dím (jūng)**. So *one o'clock* is **yāt-dím (jūng)**; *two o'clock*, however, is **léuhng-dím (jūng)**, *four o'clock* is **sei-dím (jūng)**, and so on to **saph-yih-dím (jūng)** *noon*.

TIME

1 In China, the international 24-hour clock is used in schedules for aircraft, trains, and the MTR, and in such public places as airports and stations. In daily conversations, however, the 12-hour clock is used. The hour is usually preceded by expressions that specify whether it is in the morning, afternoon, or evening. **There are two such expressions in Conversation 1. Can you find them and underline them?**

42

2 **Now, have a look at the following expressions to see if your answers are right.**

séung-jau	*in the morning*
hah-jau	*in the afternoon*
yeh-māahn	*in the evening/at night*
bun-yé	*after midnight*

V More words!

lìhng-sàhn	*midnight* (literally *zero morning*)
líhng-sàhn sahp-yih dím	*midnight 12 a.m.* (literally *zero morning 12 o'clock*)
jūng-ngh	*noon*
jūng-ngh sahp-yih dím	*12 noon* (literally *noon 12 o'clock*)

3 **In Cantonese, the time of the day always comes before the hour. Can you find two examples of this in Conversation 1? What are they?**

More on time

FĀN-JŪNG MINUTES

In Cantonese, minutes shown on the clock are **fān-jūng** (**fān** for short). So 38 minutes is **sāam-sahp-baat fān**; 5.24 is **ngh-dím yih-sahp-sei fān**; and 1.02 is **yāt-dím lìhng-yih fān** (note the use of *zero* here).

JIH FIVE MINUTES

In English, if it's 2.09 or 2.11, instead of giving the precise time, we would usually say *it's ten past two*. In Cantonese, there is a special word indicating the five-minute unit – **jih** (literally *word*), which is used in a similar way. So, we can safely say 2.09, 2.10, or 2.11 using **léuhng-dím-léuhng-go-jih** (i.e. *2 hours and 2 jih*). Theoretically, there should be twelve **jihs** (relating to clock numbers 1 to 12), but Cantonese people use only ten of them, because the sixth **jih** (number 6) is usually expressed in terms of half an hour and the twelfth **jih** (number 12) is the hour.

Whenever **jih** is used, the classifier **go** precedes it, making the time 2.10 **léuhng-dím-léuhng-go-jih** (note the pronunciation of 2, which is not **yih**, but **léuhng**), or *2 hours and 2 jih*, and 8.40 **baat-dim baat-go-jih** (*8 hours and 8 jih*).

However, in everyday conversation, you might hear Cantonese people omitting the expression **go-jih**, making the time 2.10 **leuhng-dim-yih** (note the **yih**; literally *two-hour-two*), and 8.40 **baat-dím baat** (literally *two-hour-eight*). By now, you should have figured out the rule.

BUN HALF AN HOUR

The Cantonese word for *a half-hour interval* is **bun**. What time is expressed in Conversation 1 using **bun**? Some more examples are **hah-jau sāam-dím-bun** (literally *afternoon + three-hours + half-an-hour*) for 15.30, and **sahp-dím-bun** (literally *ten-hours + half-an-hour*) for 10.30.

4 Convert the following time expressions into the Cantonese 12-hour clock.

  a 13.30   **c** 6.30 a.m.

  b 2.30 p.m. **d** 7.30 p.m.

GWĀT A QUARTER OF AN HOUR

The Cantonese for a quarter of an hour is **gwāt**, which goes with the classifier **go**. The two examples show you how it works:

6.15	**luhk-dím yāt-go gwāt**	*a quarter past six* (literally *6 hours and 1 quarter*)
6.45	**luhk-dím sām-go gwāt**	*a quarter to seven* (literally *6 hours and 3 quarters*)

Practice 1

1 04.04 **Give the following times in Cantonese and say them out loud. Remember that** *two* **can be expressed in two different ways. Which one applies here?**

a 1.00 yāt-dím (jūng)   g 7.00
b 2.00   h 8.00
c 3.00   i 9.00 gáu-dím (jūng)
d 4.00   j 10.00
e 5.00 ńgh-dím (jūng)   k 11.00
f 6.00   l 12.00

2 **Say the following in Cantonese.**
   a Morning or afternoon?
   b I would like to take the 7.30 a.m. train.
   c When will it arrive in Guangzhau?

> **LANGUAGE TIP**
> When you are confident that people will understand you, leave **jūng** out.

3 **Read the digital clocks, and translate the times into the 12-hour clock. Write the time and the day of the week down, and read them out loud. The first one has been done for you.**

a

Wednesday	Sīng-keì sāam
18.05	hah-jau luhk-dim-yāt.

b

Friday	
12.00	

c

Tuesday	
9.15	

d

Sunday	
24.00	

 Speaking

You are travelling from Hong Kong to Shanghai. Tell the **sauh-pui-yùhn** what you want in Cantonese.

a Say you want a ticket for Shanghai.
b Ask what time the first bus leaves.
c Ask what time it arrives in Shanghai.
d Say you want a return ticket.

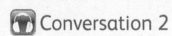 Conversation 2

04.05 *Jane lives in Cambridge, UK. She is visiting her friend Tim in Hong Kong, and is now phoning him to confirm her travel plans. Listen and answer the questions.*

1 What time is it in Cambridge when Jane phones? And in Hong Kong?

Tim	Wái?
Jane	Wái, aa-Tim àah? Ngóh haih Jane aa!
Tim	Haih-néih àah, Jane? Néih-dím aa?
Jane	Ngóh hóu-hóu. Aa-Tim, ngóh yíh-gīng jéun-beih hóu heui néih-douh laa.
Tim	Gám géi-sìh-làih āa?
Jane	Hah Sīng-kéih luhk.
Tim	Géi-dím nē?
Jane	Ngóh-wui daap lìhng-sáhn sahp-yih dím gó bāan-gēi lèih-hōi Lèuhn-dēun.
Tim	Géi-dím dou Hēung-Góng nē?
Jane	Sīng-kéih yaht seuhng-jau gáu-dím. Hēung-góng yìh-gā géi-dim aa?
Tim	Yeh-máahn baat-dím bun. Gim-kìuh nē?
Jane	Hah-jau yāt-dím bun.

> **PRONUNCIATION**
> Note the tone of the final particles: **àah** (question word with surprise) and **aa** (that is, when softening the tone, and a question word, at the end of a question).

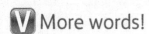 More words!

wái	*hi/hello* (for telephoning)
ngóh-wui	*I will*
Haih-néih aàh?	*Is that you?* (with surprise)
Néih-dím aa?	*How are you?* (informal, an alternative to **Néih-hóu ma?**)
Géi-sìh-làih?	*When (are you) travelling?* (literally *when-come?*)
. . . yíh-gīng jéun-beih hóu	*. . . have been ready*

2 What expressions from Conversation 2 mean the following?
   a Is that you?
   b I'm ready to go to . . . ?
   c What time is the plane?
   d When are you travelling?
   e When will you arrive?

Language discovery 2

1 Read Conversation 2 again. What is the Cantonese for the following?

  a What time is it in Hong Kong now?

  b I will take the 12 o'clock midnight plane.

If you got the answers right, congratulations! Read the answers out loud and, at the same time, pay attention to the 'time factor'.

2 Which words tell you whether the sentences are related to the past, present, or future? Try to underline the expressions that indicate time.

a	Yìh-gā Hēung-Góng haih gēi dim-jūng aa?	Present
b	Ngóh yíh-gīng júen-beih hóu heui néih-douh laa.	Past
c	Ngóh wui-dāap luhk-dím bun gó-bāan fō-chē.	Future

TIME MARKERS

Unlike English, verbs in Cantonese have only one form and do not indicate the time of an event, which is signified by time-related words/phrases. Some useful expressions are:

gām-yaht *today*	*(present)*	**seuhng-chi** *last time*	*(past)*
kàhm-yaht *yesterday*	*(past)*	**hah-chi** *next time*	*(future)*
tīng-yaht *tomorrow*	*(future)*	**yìh-gā** *now*	*(present)*
chìn-yaht *the day before yesterday*	*(past)*	**ngāam-ngāam** *just*	*(recent past)*
hauh-yaht *the day after tomorrow*	*(future)*	**tàuh-sīn** *just now*	*(recent past)*

Practice 2

1 You have to phone your Cantonese business associate John in Hong Kong to confirm his travel arrangements to London. What will you say?

You	_____?
John	Hah Sīng-kèi sāam heui néih-douh.
You	_____?
John	Ngóh-wui dāap luhk-dím-jūng gó bāan-chē.
You	_____?
John	Seuhng-jauh sahp-dím bun dou Lùhn-dūn.

2 Complete the sentences with the correct expression for the intended time.

yìh-gā	wui	yíh-gīng

a	Ngóh _____ dāap hah-jauh léuhng-dím sáam go-báan báa-sí.	Future
b	Ngóh _____ jéun-beih-hóu laa.	Past
c	_____ Beijing gēi-dō-dím aa?	Present

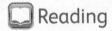

1 When she arrives at Chek-lap-gok airport in Hong Kong, Jane has no problem finding her way to where Tim is in Mongkok. But when she visits Chengdou, she finds it hard to understand the following words especially when they are displayed in simplified Chinese characters. Can you help her out? Write down the English equivalents.

出口 　　　　入口 　　　　洗手间

chēut-háu 　　yahp-háu 　　sái-sáu-gāan

_____　　_____　　_____

2 Simplified Chinese characters have been promoted in the Chinese mainland since the 1950s, and have also been adopted in Singapore and Malaysia. There are about 2,235 official simplified characters. However, Hong Kong, Macau, and Taiwan still use traditional characters. In order to understand Chinese characters around the globe, it is useful to be able to recognize both. **Try to match the following Chinese words with the English.**

	Traditional	Simplified		
a	出口		1	toilet
b	入口		2	exit
c	洗手間	洗手间	3	entrance

Writing

Jane is just in time to join her company's open day when she is back from Hong Kong. Since there are a great number of Chinese buyers visiting, her manager asks if she can write *entrance* and *exit* in Chinese to help visitors to get round the premises. Can you help her?

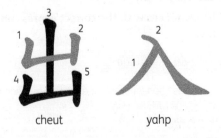

cheut 　　　　　　yahp

? Test yourself

1 Géi-dō-dím? *What time is it?* **Say them out loud.**

a	Tuesday	11.45	**e** Saturday	17.01
b	Friday	1.15	**f** Thursday	20.27
c	Sunday	6.15	**g** Wednesday	9.08
d	Monday	2.30		

2 Complete the sentences with the missing words.

a Ngóh m̀h-séung yiu dāan-chìhng-fēi. Ngóh yiu _____-fēi.

b Ngóh _____ sahp-dím-bun gó-bāan-gēi. Tīng-yaht baat-dím-jūng _____ Lèuhn-dēun.

3 04.06 **Listen to Cherry requesting travel information. Then answer the questions.**

a What time of day does Cherry want to travel?

b What are the departure times?

c What time does the second bus arrive in Guangzhau?

SELF CHECK

I CAN . . .
. . . ask for travel information.
. . . say the days of the week.
. . . confirm travel plans.
. . . ask and tell the time.

5 酒店訂房
Jáu-dim dehng-fóng
Booking a hotel room

In this unit you will learn how to:
▶ *make a hotel booking.*
▶ *write your name in Chinese characters.*
▶ *say your telephone number.*
▶ *name the month of the year.*

CEFR (A1): *Can make simple arrangements about places to stay; can spell/write one's name and give one's telephone number; can handle dates.*

 住邊度？ **jyuh bīn-douh?** *Where to stay?*

Hong Kong is famous for its impressive skyline, with over 1,200 skyscrapers forming a concrete jungle. Very often, architecture and interior design are influenced by both traditional Chinese feng-shui and modern technology. Depending on their budgets, visitors can choose from **ngh-sīng-kǎp jáu-dim** (*five-star hotels*), **bān-gún** (*guest houses*), **gūng-yuh toufóng** (*apartments*), and **léuih-gún** (*hostels*).

Those hotels which comply with the international standard are rated in terms of a five-star system. Other types of accommodation may differ in what they offer. Before booking a room, it may be a wise move to ask **Hó-m̀h hó-yíh tái-hah gāan-fóng aa?** (*May I see the room?*).

Jóu-chāan (*breakfast*) is usually included in most hotels, but, to be on the safe side, you'd better ask in advance **Bāau-m̀h-bāau jóu-chāan aa?** (*Is breakfast included?*). It is highly unlikely that **ngh-chāan** (*lunch*) and **máahn-chāan** (*supper*) will be provided free.

 What four types of accommodation are mentioned in the article? Underline the Cantonese words for these.

Vocabulary builder

05.01 Read the expressions and fill in the missing English words. Then listen to the audio and imitate the speaker.

酒店房間 *JÁU-DIM FÒHNG-GĀAN* HOTEL ROOM

房	fóng (short for fòhng-gaan)	*room*
訂房	dehng-fóng	*room booking* (literally *book room*)
預訂	yuh-dehng	*reservation*
雙人房	sēung-yàhn fóng	*double room*
單人房	dāan-yàhn fóng	*single* _____
套房	tou-fóng	*en suite*
洗手間	sái-sáu gāan	*toilet*
有浴室	yáuh yuhk-sāt	*have bathroom*
無浴室	móuh yuhk-sāt	*no* _____
包早餐	bāau jóu-cāan	literally *include breakfast*
唔包早餐	m̀h-báau jóu-cáan	literally *not include* _____

> **PRONUNCIATION**
> Note the tone of **fóng**, which is short for **fòhng-gaan**.

生詞 *SĀANG-CHÌH* NEW EXPRESSIONS

十月五號	Sahp-yuht ńgh-houh.	*5th October*
住幾晚呢?	Jyuh géi-máahn nē?	*How many nights will you be staying?* (literally *Live for how many days?*)
點寫呀?	Dím-sé aa?	*How do you write?*
幾多號?	Géi-dō houh?	*What is the number?*
電話	dihn-wá	*telephone*
手機	sáu-gēi (short for sáu-tàih dihn-wa)	*mobile phone*
同埋	tùhng-màaih	*and*
要有	yiu-yáuh	literally *must have*
總共	júng-guhng	*total; in total*
你個姓	néih-go sing	*your surname*
中文姓林	jūng-màhn sing-làhm	*surname is 'Lam' in Chinese*
雙木林	sēung-muhk làhm	*a description of how the surname 'Lam' (forest) is written in Chinese*
唔該晒	m̀h-gōi-saai	*thank you* (for a service)
英國劍橋	Yīng-gwok Gim-Kìuh	*Cambridge, UK*

> **PRONUNCIATION**
> Note the pronunciation and tone differences between **ńgh** (the number *five*; nasal) and **m̀h** (*no, negation*; lips closed).

CLASSIFIERS USED IN THIS UNIT

間	gāan	*for a room, hotel, and house, etc.*
	yāt-gāan fóng	*a room*
條	tìuh	*for longish objects; see Unit 3*
	yāt-tiuh sìh	*a key*

> **PRONUNCIATION**
> Note the tone of **sìh** (*key*), which is the same as **sìh-gāan** (*time*).

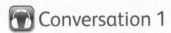# Conversation 1

05.02 *Samantha Forrest phones Dūng-fōng-jī-jyū (the Pearl of the Orient), a guest house in Hong Kong, to book a room. A jip-doih-yùhn (hotel receptionist) answers her.*

1 How many nights does she wish to stay?

Jip-doih-yùhn	Jóu-sàhn, Dūng-fōng-jī-jyū.
Samantha	Jóu-sàhn, ngóh-séung dehng-gāan fóng.
Jip-doih-yùhn	Bīn-yát nē?
Samantha	Sahp-yuht ngh-houh.
Jip-doih-yùhn	Sēung-yàhn fóng?
Samantha	M̀h-haih, Ngóh-séung yiu-gāan dāan-yàhn fóng.
	Yiu-yáuh sái-sáu-gāan tùhng-màaih yuhk-sāt ge.
Jip-doih-yùhn	Jyuh géi-dō máahn aa?
Samantha	Ngh-máahn, gāan-fóng géi-dō chín nē?
Jip-doih-yùhn	Yāt-máahn yih-baak ngh-sahp-mān góng-jí, júng-guhng yāt-chīn yih-baak ngh-sahp mān.
Samantha	Bāau-m̀h-bāau jóu-chāan nē?
Jip-doih-yùhn	Bāau jóu-chāan. Chéng-mahn gwai-sing?
Samantha	Samantha Forrest
Jip-doih-yùhn	Néih-go sing dím-chyun aa?
Samantha	F-o-r-r-e-s-t. Jūng-mán sing-làhm, sēung-muhk làhm.
Jip-doih-yùhn	M̀h-gōi saai, néih-go-dihn-wá géi-dō houh nē?
Samantha	Yīng-gwōk Gim-kíuh 01223 264 32.

PRONUNCIATION
Note the tone differences between **sēung** (*double*) and **séung** (*want*).

PRONUNCIATION
Note the tone differences between **mān** (*dollar*), **mán** (*language*; as in **Jūng-mán**, *Chinese*), and **mahn** (literally *ask*, as in **chéng-mahn**, literally *please ask*, but when the two words are used together it means *excuse me!*).

2 Match the questions and answers.

a Séunng-yàhn fóng?   1 Luhk-baak sāam-sahp mān góng-baih.
b Géi-dō máahn?   2 M̀h-haih, dāan-yàhn fóng.
c Gāan-fóng géi-chín aa?   3 F-o-r-r-e-s-t
d Néih-go sing dím-sé aa?   4 Jyuh ngh-máahn.

3 Read the conversation and answer the following questions.

a What type of room does Samantha want?
b How much is the room per night?
c Is breakfast included?

4 05.03 **Now listen to the lines from the conversation and repeat. Then listen to the receptionist's lines and answer as if you were Samantha.**

LANGUAGE TIP
Telephone numbers in Cantonese are usually given in single digits.

Language discovery 1

What words/phrases have been used in Conversation 1 to express the following?

    a I would like to . . .
    b and
    c in total

> 輪到你 **LÈUHN-DOU-LÉH** *YOUR TURN*
> Can you say *I would like to book a room* in Cantonese?

1 *I would like to . . .* or *I want to . . .* is translated as **Ngóh-séung . . .** *I would like to buy . . .* is therefore **Ngóh-séunng máaih . . .** (see Unit 2), and *I would like to have . . .* is **Ngóh-séung yiu . . .**

2 *And* is translated as **tùhng-màaih**. The phrase *toilet and bathroom* is therefore **sái-sáu-gāan tùhng-màaih yuhk-sāt**.

3 *Total* is translated as **júng-gúng**. *A total of HK$1,250* is therefore **júng-gùng yāt-chīn yih-baak ngóh-sahp mān**.

> 輪到你 **LÈUHN-DOU-LÉH**
> Can you say aloud the phrase *a total of US$635* in Cantonese?

月份 *YUHT-FAHN* THE MONTHS

月   **yuht**   *month*, short for **yuht-fahn**

The words for the months are very straightforward in Cantonese. Can you see the pattern? Complete the following list.

一月	yāt-yuht	*January*	七月	chāt-yuht	_____
二月	yih-yuht	_____	八月	baat-yuht	_____
三月	sáam-yuht	_____	九月	gáu-yuht	_____
四月	sei-yuht	_____	十月	sahp-yuht	_____
五月	ngóh-yuht	_____	十一月	sahp-yāt-yuht	_____
六月	luhk-yuht	_____	十二月	sahp-yih yuht	*December*

日期 *YAHT-KÈIH* DAY OF THE MONTH

To express the date we say **yuht** (*month*) first and then **yaht** (*day*) or **houh** (*number*, which is more common). So in the following examples, **houh** precedes **yaht**:

yāt-yuht yāt-houh/yaht	*1st January* (literally *one month one number/day*)
ngóh-yuht ngóh-houh/yaht	*5th May* (literally *five month five number/day*)
saph-yih-yuht yih-saph-ngóh houh/yaht	*25th December* (literally *twelve month twenty-five number/day*)

QUESTIONS

It is common to start a question with **Nèih-go** (*yours, your* + classifier **go**) as in:

Nèih-go méng dím-sé aa? (Ask someone how to write his/her Chinese name.)
Néih-go sáu-gēi géi-dō houh aa? (Ask someone's mobile number.)

 Note the scenario in Conversation 1: the **jip-doih-yùhn** (*hotel receptionist*) asks Samantha how to spell her surname. Samantha does not only spell it out, she also tells the receptionist how to write her Chinese surname, which is **Làmh** (Lam, literally *forest*). The Chinese character 林 is a combination of two identical characters 木 **muhk** (*wood, tree*). The ideogram means two 'trees' forming a forest, which is exactly what the expression **sēung-muhk làhm** means. Unlike the English alphabet, Chinese characters can only be **sé** (*written*), not spelt. Therefore we can ask people to write their names, not spell them: **Nèih-go méng dim-sé aa?** However, if we ask someone to spell their name, we use the phrase **Néih-go méng dim-chyun aa?**

 ## Practice 1

1 Match the Cantonese with the English.

 a Néih gwai-sing?   **1** What's your email address?
 b Néih-dihn-wá géi-dō houh nē? **2** What's your surname?
 c Néih-go dihn-yàuh haih?   **3** What's your telephone number?

2 Translate the following dates into Cantonese.

 a 24th February   **b** 7th July   **c** 25th December

 ## Listen and understand

05.04 Listen and make a note of the telephone numbers you hear.

 a Tel. _____
 b Tel. _____
 c Tel. _____, extension _____

> **LANGUAGE TIP**
> Géi-houh nē? is short for géi-do houh nē?

> **PRONUNCIATION**
> Note the tone differences between **gēi** as in **sau-gēi** (*mobile phone*) and **géi** as in **géi-houh** (*What number?*).

Speaking

Answer these questions about yourself.

 a Néih-go sing dím-chyun aa?   **c** Néih-go dihn-wá géi houh nē?
 b Néih-go méng dím-duhk aa?   **d** Néih-go sáu-gēi géi houh-nē?

54

Conversation 2

At the Hotel Viceroy in Macau, the jip-doih-yùhn (hotel receptionist) is busy attending to a number of new arrivals.

1 Listen to the conversation. Is the hotel booked up? How can you tell?

Guest 1	Néih-hóu, ngóh dehng-jó gāan sēung-yàhn fóng. Haih béi ngóh tùhng-màaih ngóh go-néui ge.
Jip-doih-yuhn	Haih-yuhng mē-méng dāng-gei nē?
Guest 1	Wohng Pui-lìhng.
Jip-doih-yuhn	Nī-dī haih dehng-fóng jī-líu. Mh-gōi-néih hái nī-douh chīm-méng. Júng-gung haih ngh-baak baat-sahp mān. Nī-tìuh sóu-sìh hái-néih gāan-fóng ge.
Guest 1	Mh-gōi-saai.
Guest 2	Mh-gōi néih. Gām-yaht juhng yáuh-móuh fóng-hūng aa?
Jip-doih-yuhn	Deui-mh-jyuh. Móuh-laa. Jáu-dim chyùhn-múhn.

More words!

dehng-jó	*booked*
béi	*give*
juhng	*still*
dāng-gei	*register; booked-in in this context*
dehng-fóng jī-líu	*room-booking information*
sóu-sìh	*key*
hūng	*empty*
chyùhn-múhn	*full (literally completely full)*

> **DON'T FORGET**
> **tìuh** is a classifier for *key*.

2 Match the Cantonese phrases from Conversation 2 with the English.

a Haih b ngóh tùhng-màaih ngóh go-néoi.   1 In what name?
b Ngóh dehng-jó gāan fóng.   2 For me and my daughter.
c Haih-yuhng mē-méng dāng-gēi nē?   3 I have a room booked.

💡 Language discovery 2

What is the Cantonese for the following in Conversation 2?

a I have booked a double room.
b Is there any room for today?

咗 -JÓ

-jó (*has/have been*) indicates an action that has been completed. It cannot be used on its own and must follow a verb, and is therefore preceded by a hyphen in Cantonese romanization. Some examples are:

dehng-jó tói	*have booked a table*
máaih-jó jēung gēi-piu	*have bought a plane ticket*

重 JUHNG

Juhng has such multiple meanings as *in addition* and *furthermore*, but in this unit, it means *still* and *yet*:

Juhng yiu dehng-tói!	*(I) still need to book the table!*
Juhng yáuh-móuh gēi-piu aa?	*(Do you) still have the plane ticket?*

SINGULAR AND PLURAL

In Cantonese, nouns remain the same whether they are singular or plural. There is no need to add **-s** or **-es** to the end of the word. For example:

léuhng jēung gēi-piu	*two train tickets*
ńgh-tìuh gwàhn	*five skirts*
baat-gāan fóng	*eight rooms*

1 Complete the sentences with the correct actions.

dehng-jó	chīm-méng	muhn	yáuh-móuh

a Ngóh _____ gāan sēung-yàhn fóng.
b Gām-yaht juhng _____ fōng-hūng aa?
c Chéng-néih hái nī-douh _____.
d Jáu-dim cyùhn _____.

2 Complete these phrases with the correct classifier.

a Léuhng _____ dāan-yàhn fóng. (tìuh/gāan)
b Sāam _____ sóu-sìh. (tìuh/gāan)
c Yāt _____ yuhk sāt. (tìuh/gāan)

Speaking

You want to spend a week in Shanghai. Use what you know to speak to the hotel receptionist.

a Ask if they have a double room for 15th June, for a week.
b Ask how much the room costs.
c Ask if breakfast is included.

 Reading

Here is a hotel room with various facilities for its guests. First match the Chinese with the English, using the pictures to help you. Then write down the appropriate English/Chinese terms in the blanks provided.

Traditional	Simplified		
a 電話	电话	1	free internet
b 淋浴		2	telephone
c 免費互聯網	免费互联网	3	shower

? Test yourself

1 05.06 **Listen and note the booking details you hear.**

   a Sing-mìhng?
   b Dihn-wā houh-mā?
   c Fòhng-gāan leuih-biht?
   d Dou-daht yaht-kèih?
   e Jyuh géi-máahn?

LANGUAGE TIP
leuih-biht *type*;
dou-daht *arrival*

> **PRONUNCIATION**
> Note the tone difference between **fóhng-gāan** (*room*) and **yāt-gāan-fóng** (*one room*).

2 **What questions would you ask to get these replies?**

   a M̀h-haih, ngóh-séung yiu-gāan sēung-yàhn fóng.
   b Néih-gāan séung-yàhn fóng júng-guhng HKD 1,250.
   c Yīng-gwōk Gīm-kìuh 01223 264 32.
   d Deui-m̀h-jyuh. Jáu-dim chyùhn-múhn.

SELF CHECK	
I CAN . . .	
○	. . . make a hotel booking.
○	. . . give my telephone number.
○	. . . say the months of the year.

6

點樣去？
Dím-yéung heui?
How to get there?

In this unit you will learn how to:

▶ *ask for and give directions.*
▶ *ask and say how far a place is.*
▶ *give your address.*
▶ *ask how to get somewhere by public transport.*

CEFR: *Can ask for and give directions; can get simple information about travel using public transport; can give his/her address.*

游覽 Yàuh-láahm *Sightseeing*

Hong Kong is not just good for shopping. In the city and its **lèih-dóu** (*outlying islands*), there is much to see and do. **Bok-maht-gún** (*museums*) are plentiful, as are century-old buildings and monuments, together with **màhn-faa gú-jīk** (*cultural relics*). Lovers of geology would no doubt wish to see the **deih-jāt gūng-yún** (*Global Geopark of China*), opened in 2009. Historians would not want to miss the **chēut-tóu mành-maht** (*archaeological finds*) at the Li Cheng Uk Han tomb. Equally intriguing is the **wàih-chyūn** (*Walled Village*) in Fanling.

To help you get around, these are useful Cantonese expressions: **M̀h-gōi néih, chíng-mahn dím-heui [Sīng-gwōng-daaih-douh] nē?** (*Excuse me, how can I get to [the Avenue of Stars]?*); **Chíng-mahn [sái-sāu gāan] haih-bīn-douh aa?** (*Could you please tell me where [the toilets] are?*); **Haih-m̀h-haih hóu-yúhn gaa?** (*Is it far?*); **Fuh-gahn yáuh-móuh [leúih-hāak séun-maahn zūng-sām] nē?** (*Is there [a tourist information centre] nearby?*)

What words in the text mean *far, nearby,* and *How can I get to . . . ?*

Vocabulary builder

06.01 **Look at the following phrases used in the dialogue and fill in the missing English words. Try pronouncing each word on your own. Then, listen to the audio and try to imitate the speakers as closely as you can.**

方向 *FÔNG-HOENG* DIRECTIONS

呢度	nī-douh	*here*
嗰度	gó-douh	*there*
喺邊度？	Haih bīn-douh?	*Where?*
佢地喺邊度？	Kéuih-deih hái bīn-douh?	_____ *are they?*
係唔係好近？	Haih-m̀h-haih hóu-gáhn?	*Is it close (to here)?*
喺左邊	hái jó-bihn	*on the left*
喺右邊	hái yauh-bihn	*on the* _____

市中心 *SÍH-JŪNG-SĀM* AROUND TOWN

銀行	ngáhn-hòhng	*bank*	大廈	daaih-hah	*building*
藥房	yeuhk-fòhng	*chemist's*	街市	gāai-síh	*market*
教堂	gaau-tóng	*church*	廣場	gwóng-chèuhng	*square*
戲院	hei-yún	*cinema*	巴士總站	bā-sí júng-jaahm	___ *terminus*

NEW EXPRESSIONS

點樣去…？	Dīm-yéung heui …?	*How to get to …?*
附近有無…？	Fuh-gahn yáuh-móuh …?	*Is there …nearby?*
喺街尾	hái gāai-máih	*at the end of the street*
喺隔籬…	hái … gaak-lèih	*next to …*
喺呢條街	Hái nī-tìuh gāai …	*On this street …*
喺呢度行去	Hái nī-douh hàahng-heui	*walk from here*
對面係…	deui-mihn haih …	*opposite is …*
向前走	heung-chìhn jáu	*go straight on …*
就到	jauh-douh	*soon arrive, will arrive*
轉左	jyun-jó	*turn left*
轉右	jyun-yauh	*turn right*
街角	gāai-gok	*street corner*
第三個街口	daih sáam-go gáai-hauh	*take the third street*
好近啫	hóu-káhn jēk	*very near*
近住…嗰度	gahn-jyuh…. gó-douh	*near … there*

PARTICLES INTRODUCED IN THIS UNIT

啫	jēk	*no more than, only*
嘞	laak	*that's how it is* (see *Complete Cantonese*)

CLASSIFIERS INTRODUCED IN THIS UNIT

盞	jáan	for lamp or light
	yāt-jáan hùhng-luhk dāng	*a traffic light* (literally *a red-green light*)

Conversation 1

06.02 *Robert is trying to find his way in Kowloon.*

1 Listen to the conversation between Robert and the jip-doih-yùhn. How many places is Robert trying to find?

Robert	Deui-m̀h-jyuh, chéng-mahn fuh-gahn yáuh-móuh ngàhn-hòhng aa?
Jip-doih-yùhn	Yáuh, Nèih-dēun-douh yáuh yāt gáan, hái gáai-máih, deui-mihn haih gáai-síh.
Robert	Dím-yéung-heui aa?
Jip-doih-yùhn	Hái nī-tìuh gāai heung-chìhn jáu, daih sāam-gō gāai-háu jyun-jó.
Robert	M̀h-gōi-saai, gám bok-mat-gúhn hái bīn-douh nē?
Jip-doih-yùhn	Gahn-jyuh gaau-tóng gó-douh, hái hei-yuhn gaak-lèih.
Robert	Haih-m̀h-haih hóu-yúhn aa?
Jip-doih-yùhn	M̀h-haih hóu-yuhn. Haih nī-douh hàahng-heui ńgh-fān-jūng jauh-dou.
Robert	Dím hàahng nē?
Jip-doi-yun	Hàahng-dou gāai-gok, jyun-yauh, bok-maht-gūn jauh-hái gó-douh.
Robert	M̀h-gōi-saai.

> **LANGUAGE TIP**
> **Káhn** (*near*) is an informal alternative to **gáhn**. *Very near* is **hóu-káhn**, not **hóu-gáhn**. The Chinese character 近 is the same for both **káhn** and **gáhn**

> **PRONUNCIATION**
> Note the tone difference between **hái** (*to be in/at*; *in/at* a place or time) and **haih** (*is/am/are/to be*)

2 Match the Chinese with the English.

a	Hái-bīn-douh?	1	There is one.
b	Haih-m̀h-haih hóu-yúhn aa?	2	Is there a bank nearby?
c	Yáuh yāt-gāan.	3	It's near.
d	Hóu káhn-jēk.	4	It's next to the cinema.
e	Fu-gahn jauh-móuh ngàhn-hòhng aa?	5	Where is it?
f	Hái hei-yún gaak-lèih.	6	Is it far?

3 Read the conversation and answer the questions.

  a What's at the end of Nathan Road (*Nèih-dēun-douh*)?
  b What's next to the cinema?
  c How far is the museum?
  d How do you get to the museum?

4 06.03 **Now listen to the lines from the conversation and repeat. Then listen to Robert's questions and respond as if you were the receptionist.**

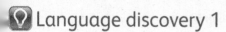

Language discovery 1

Go back to Conversation 1, and find the Cantonese for the following expressions:

a Is there a bank ... ?
b Where is the museum?

有無 *YÁUH-MÓUH* AGAIN! (see Unit 2)

To start a question with *Is/Are there ... ?*, use **Yáuh-móuh ... ?**

To say *there is/are ...* , use **yáuh ...** , and to say *there isn't/aren't*, use **móuh ...**

Q Fu-gahn yáuh-móuh chīu-kāp   sīh-chèuhng?   *Is there a supermarket nearby?*

A Yáuh sāam-gāan   *Yes, there are three.*

A Móuh, yāt-gāan dōu móuh.   *No, not a single one.*

邊度 *BĪN-DOUH*, 呢度 *NĪ-DOUH*, 嗰度 *GÓ-DOUH*

When asking about where something is located, use **bīn-douh** (*where*). Unlike the English word *where*, **bīn-douh** can either be put at the beginning or at the end of a question, as in these examples:

Bīn-douh haih gāai-sih?   or   **Gāai-sih hái-bīn-douh?**
Where is the market? (literally *Market is where?*)

Bīn-douh-haih hei-yún?   or   **Hei-yún hái-bīn-douh?**
Where is the cinema? (literally *Cinema is where?*)

> **LANGUAGE TIP**
> Note **haih** and **hái**: when **bīn-douh** is put at the beginning of the sentence, it is followed by **haih** as in **Bīn-douh-haih ...** When **bīn-douh** is used at the end of the sentence, it is preceded by **hái**, as in **... hái-bīn-douh.**

In Cantonese, we often use the vague expressions **nī-douh** (*here*) and **gó-douh** (*there*) to indicate where things are. Those two expressions are usually preceded by **hái**, as follows:

Q Hei-yún hái-bīn-douh?   *Where is the cinema?*

A Hái-nī-douh.   *It's here.*

Hái-gó-douh.   *It's there.*

If we reword the question to **Bīn-douh haih hei-yún?**, we can still use the same answer **Hái nī-douh** and **Hái gó-douh**.

To be more specific about locations, we can use the following expressions:

hái gāak-lèih	*it's next door*
hái jāk-bihn	*it's beside (you)* (literally *by the side*)
hái chình-mihn	*it's at the front* (literally *at the front-face*)
hái hauh-mihn	*it's at the back* (literally *at the back-face*)
hái yahp-mihn	*it's inside* (literally *at the inside-face*)
hái chēut-mihn	*it's outside* (literally *at the outside-face*)

GWO . . . JAUH DOUH

To say that a place is a few blocks from here, one way is to start the sentence with **gwo** (*past*) and end the sentence with **jauh-douh** (*soon arrive*). There is no need to mention *here* in such an expression. Examples:

Gwo leuhng-gāan jauh-douh.
It's about two blocks from here.
literally *Walk past two blocks it will be there.*

Ngàhn-hòhng? Gwo sāam-tiuh gāai jauh-dou.
The bank? It's three streets away from here.
literally *The bank? Walk past three streets it will be there.*

DÍM-YÉUNG HEUI? HÁI-BĪN DOUH?

There are two ways of asking where a place is using either **dím-yéung heui?** or **hái-bīn-douh?** For example, if you want to enquire how to go to the cinema, you can say:

Hei-yún dím-yéung heui?	literally *cinema how to go?*
Dím-yéung heui hei-yún?	literally *how to go cinema?*

However, **hái-bīn-douh** can only be used at the end of a sentence:

Hei-yu hái-bīn-douh?	literally *cinema where is it?*

DAAIH-KOI . . . JAUH-DOU

To give an approximate distance, we can start the sentence with **daaih-koi** (*about*) and end with **jauh-dou** (*soon arrive*):

Daaih-koi léuhng-go jūng-tàuh jauh-douh.	*It's about two hours away.*
Daaih-koi léuhng-baak maih jauh-douh.	*It's about two hundred metres away.*

GIVING DIRECTIONS

When giving directions, no tense markers are needed. The following expressions will be useful:

heung-chìhn jáu	*go forward*
heung-chìhn jihk-jáu	*go straight on*
hái daih-yih go gāai-háu jyun-jó	*turn right at the second street* (literally *at the second street-mouth turn left*)

FIRST, SECOND, THIRD

In Unit 2, we learned to say *one, two, three*, etc. as **yāt**, **yih**, **sāam**, and so on. However, to say *the first/second/third street* in Cantonese, we need to add **daih** (*the*) before the numbers. So:

daih-yāt/yih/sāam tiuh-gāai	*the first/second/third street*
daih-yāt/yih/sāam/jáan hùhng-luhk dāng	*the first/second/third traffic light*
daih-yāt/yih/sāam/ go jyun-gok	*the first/second/third corner*

> **DON'T FORGET**
> **Tiuh** is a classifier (see Unit 3). It goes with **gāai** (*street*).

Practice 1

1 **Give the Cantonese for the following sentences.**

   a It's about five blocks from here.
   b It's about six hours away.
   c It's some 8,000 kilometres (**máih**) away.

2 **Turn the following words into questions using dím-yéung heui and hái-bīn douh. The first one has been done for you.**

   a yeuhk-fòhng
      Dím-yéung-heui yeuhk-fòhng?
      Yeuhk-fòhng dím-yéung-heui?
      Yeuhk-fòhng hái-bīn douh?
   b Sō-hòuh
   c Léuih-haak sēun-maahn jūng-sām
   d Màhn-móuh-míu

3 **Complete the Cantonese translation, then read the sentences out loud.**

   a The bank is next to the church, about two minutes away.
      Ngàhn-hòhng hái Gaau-tóng _____, daaih-koi léuhng-fān-jūng
      _____.
   b The museum is opposite the market, about a hundred metres away.
      _____ jauh-haih gāai-síh _____, daaih-koih yāt-baak-máih _____.
   c The bus-terminus is on the right.
      _____ hái _____ bihn.

4 **Match the Cantonese with the English sentences.**

   a Gaau-tóng jauh haih gāai-máaih.   **1** The cinema is near the hotel.
   b Bā-sí júng-jaahm haih gaai-si   **2** The bus terminus is next
      gaak-lei.   to the market.
   c Hei-yún jauh-haih jāu-dim   **3** The church is at the end of
      fuh-gahn.   this street.

5 **Complete the sentences with the words from the list.**

jyun	heung	chìhn-mihn	gāak-lèih

   a _____ chíhn jāu dou gāai-méih, _____ yauh.
   b Hei-yún jauh-hái ngàhn-hòhng _____.
   c Daaih-yāt go gāai-hàu _____ jó.
   d Fó-cē-jaahm jauh-hái _____.

 Conversation 2

06.04 Jenny, Robert's friend, invites him to her Happy Valley home on Hong Kong Island.

1 Listen to the conversation. What transport can Robert take to Jenny's place?

Robert	Néih-jyuh hái bīn-douh aa?
Jenny	Mē-wá?
Robert	Néih-ge deih-jí nē?
Jenny	Páau-máh déi, bāat-sahp-bāat houh, sāam-lóu, B joh.
Robert	Ngóh-dím-làih néih-douh aa? Daap deih-tit? Daap bāa-sí? Dihng-haih hàahng-louh nē?
Jenny	Néih-jyuh-hái bīn-gāan jáu-dim aa?
Robert	Ngóh-jyuh-hái Wàh-Mèih-Laih, Nèih-dēun-douh, gahn-jyuh deih-tit jaahm.
Jenny	Gám néih dāap-deih-tit lāa. Háih Tuhng-lòh-wāan-jaahm lohk-chē. Gwo sāam-tìuh-gāai jauh-douh laa.
Robert	Néih hó-m̀h-hó-yí jou-góng yāt-ci néih-go deih-ji aa?
Jenny	Páau-máh-déi, bāat-sahp-bāat houh, sāam-lóu, B joh.

> **PRONUNCIATION**
>
> Note the tone difference between **deih** as in **deih-jí** (*address*) and **déi** as in **Páau-máh-déi** (*Happy Valley*).

ⓥ More words!

Néih-jyuh háih bīn-douh?	*Where do you live?*
Néih-ge deih-jí nē?	*What is your address?*
Mē-wá?	*What? What did you say? (literally What spoken language?)*

Wàh-méih-laih is short for *Hotel Waa-Mei-Lai.*

Néih-dēun-douh is *Nathan Road.*

2 Listen to the conversation again, and answer the following questions.

    a Where is Hotel Wáh-méih-laih?

    b How far is Páau-máh-déi from the underground?

💡 Language discovery 2

Find the phrases in the conversation that mean:

a What's your address? (There are two possible answers)
b 88 Happy Valley, third floor, flat B.
c I'm at Hotel Wáh-méih-laih.

CARDINAL NUMBERS

When referring to floor numbers, Cantonese simply uses cardinal numbers. So, *the first floor* is **yāt-lóu**; *the second floor* is **yih-lóu**, *the eleventh floor* is **sahp-yāt lóu**, and *the twenty-fifth floor* is **yih-sahp-ngh lóu**.

🔓 Practice 2

1 06.05 Listen and note the addresses that you hear.

a _____
b _____
c _____

> **LANGUAGE TIP**
> **Sāt** (*room*) is an alternative to **joh**.

2 Re-order the sentences into a dialogue. Begin with 1.

___ Haih-m̀h-haih hóu-káhn bók-māt-gún gáa?
_1_ Ngóh dím-yéung heui bok-maht-gún nē? Daap deih-tit dihng-hái haahng-louh aa?
___ Néih hó-yíh daap Jūng-wàahn-sin.
___ Néih hó-yíh daap deih-tit.
___ Daap bīn-tíuh-sin nē?
___ Haih-aa, hóu-káhn gaa. Gwó léuhng-tìuh gāai jauh-dou laak.

3 Can you say the following floors in Cantonese? The first sentence is done for you.

a I live on the ninth floor. **Ngóh jyuh-hái gáu lóu.**
b I live on the third floor.
c I live on the sixteenth floor.
d I live on the twenty-first floor.

4 Put the sentences in order to show the proper directions.

a jauh-hái / gaak-lèih / Ngáhn-hòhng / yeuhk-fòhng /
b jauh-douh laa / sāam-tìuh gāai / Gwo
c daih sei-gān / Hái nī-tìuh gāai / jauh-haih laa / heung chìhn-jóu.

Reading

Jenny has invited Robert to her home for dinner. In case Robert cannot find his way, she has emailed him her address in Chinese:

From: Jenny
Date: 23 September
To: Robert
Subject: my address

Hi Robert

跑馬地, 八十八號, 三樓, B座 / 跑马地, 八十八号, 三楼, B座

Páau-máh déi, bāat-sahp-bāat houh, sāam-lóu, B joh.

Happy Valley, third floor, flat B

Jenny

Like Jenny, most people in Hong Kong live in a flat. The city is not big, and there is no need to have postcodes. To make sure the address is clear for its purpose, one needs to include such details as the area, name of street, name of building (if there is any), floor, and room number.

Jenny's address is a simplified version. Read it carefully and try to match the English with the Chinese words.

a 地區 / 地区 deih-kēui (*area*)　　　**1** B座

b 層數 / 层数 chàahn-sou (*floor*)　　**2** 跑馬地 / 跑马地

c 室號 / 室号 sāt-houh (*flat number*)　**3** 三樓 / 三楼

Speaking

How would you ask these questions in Cantonese?

a What's your address?
b Is it far?
c Can you repeat the address?
d How do I get there?

? Test yourself

1 **Complete the sentences with one of these words:**

fuh-guhn	hauh-mihn	haih-bīn douh	dím-heui

a Deui-m̀h-jyuh, Faai-Lohk jáu-dim _____ nē?

b _____ yáuh-móuh bōk-maht-gún aa?

c M̀h-gōi leíh, yeuhk-fòhng _____ aa?

d Hei-yún hái gwóng-chèuhng _____.

 2 06.06 **Listen and note the answers to the following questions.**

a Deui-m̀h jyuh, gāai-síh háai bīn-douh aa?

b M̀h-gōi, bā-síh júng-jaahm hái bīn-douh nē?

c Síu-jé, chíhng-mahn fuh-gahn yaúh-móuh yeuhk-fòhng aa?

d Sīn-sāang, chíhng-mahn hei-yúhn káhn-m̀h-káhn nē-douh nē?

 3 **It is your first day in Macau. Try to speak to the tourist information desk.**

You	*Where is Daaih-Sām-bā pàaih-fōng?*
Jip-doih-yùhn	Daaih-Sām-bā pàaih-fōng hái Daaih-gwóng-chèuhng fu-gahn.
You	*Is it far?*
Jip-doih-yùhn	M̀h-haih houh-yúhn jēk. Hái nī-douh hàang-heui ngh-fān-jūng jauh-dou.
You	*How do I get there?*
Jip-doih-yùhn	Heung-cìhn jáu, daih yih-go gāai-háu jyun-jó.
You	*Thank you. Is there a bank nearby?*
Jip-doih-yùhn	Yáuh-aa. Hái nī-tìuh gāai heung cìhn-jóu, daih sei-gān jauh-haih laa.

Daaih-sām-bā pàaih-fōng is the famous ruin of Macau's St Paul's Cathedral.

Daaih-gwóng-chèuhng (*big square*) is an informal way of referring to Macau's Sanado Square.

SELF CHECK

I CAN . . .
. . . ask for and give directions.
. . . ask and say how far a place is.
. . . give my address.
. . . ask how to get somewhere by public transport.

1 **Write down the Cantonese transcription of the following times, and then say them out loud in Cantonese.**
   a three fifteen   c eight forty-five
   b a quarter to four   d two fifteen

   Points: _____ /4

2 **Write the following times in Cantonese. Then read them out loud. a and e have been done for you:**
   a 3 a.m. bun-yé sāam-dím   e 9 p.m. yeh-máahn gáu-dím
   b 6 p.m.   f 2 a.m.
   c 8 a.m.   g 11 p.m.
   d 5 p.m.   h 10 a.m.

   Points: _____ /6

3 **Say the following times using the 12-hour clock with such expressions as seuhng-jau, hah-jau, lihng-sàn, and fān. The first sentence has been done for you.**
   a Fēi-gē seuhng-jau sahp-dim ngh-sahp-fān (10.50) hōi, hah-jau léuhng-dím-sāam-sahp-fān (14.30) dou Bāk-gīng.
   b Bā-sí _____ (8.15) hōi, _____ (18.20) dou Sām-jàn.
   c Fó-cē _____ (14.00) hōi, _____ (16.00) dou Gwóng-jàu.
   d Syùhn _____ (0.00) hōi, _____ (7.00) dou Ou-mún.

   Points: _____ /6

4 **Say the following in Cantonese. Use such expressions as lìhng, jih, gwāt, and go, etc. The first two have been done for you.**
   a 1.15 yāt-dím yāt-go-gwāt   g 3.45
   b 2.30 léuhng-dím bun   h 4.05
   c 1.10   i 3.15
   d 4.20   j 5.25
   e 7.35   k 9.45
   f 10.50   l 11.55

   Points: _____ /12

5 R2.01 **Man-git wants to go to Guangzhau. He talks to sauh-piu yùhn (*the person at the ticket office*). Listen and complete the missing words.**

Man-git	Ṁh-gōi néih, ngóh-séung _____ heui Gwóng-jāu ge fó-chē fēi.
Sauh-piu yùhn	Bīn-yaht nē?
Man-git	_____-houh, Sīng-kèih _____.
Sauh-piu yùhn	_____ dihng-hahi _____ ne?
Man-git	Seung-jau laa. _____ go-bāan chē haih _____ aa?
Sauh-piu yùhn	Seung-jau _____ yáuh yāt-bāan

Points: _____ /8

6 R2.02 **Yuk-ling wants a hotel room. She talks to the jip-doih-yùhn (*hotel receptionist*). Listen and fill in each blank with an appropriate expression.**

Yuk-ling	Ngóh séung-hái _____ yiu gāan-fóng.
Jip-doih-yùhn	Yiu _____?
Yuk-ling	Ṁh-haih, _____.
Jip-doih-yùhn	_____ nē?
Yuk-ling	_____ laa.

Points: _____ /4

7 Translate the following sentences into Cantonese, and then read them out.

- **a** I have booked a double-room.
- **b** I have bought two shirts.
- **c** I still want to go to Beijing.
- **d** Do you have any train tickets?
- **e** Is breakfast included?
- **f** What is the total cost?

Points: _____ /6

8 Match the Cantonese phrases with the English.

- **a** Turn right at the fifth street.
- **b** Where is Hotel Waa-mei-lai?
- **c** Is there a supermarket nearby?
- **d** The toilet is over there.

- **1** Sái-sáu-gāan hái go-douh.
- **2** Fuh-gaahn yáuh-móuh chīu-kāp-sih-chéuhng nē?
- **3** Daih nǵh-go gāai-háu jyun-yauh.
- **4** Wah-méih-laih jāu-dim hái-bīn nē?

Points: _____ /4

9 Complete the following sentences with either gwo or daaih-koi.

- **a** chīu-kāp-sih-chéuhng? _____ léuhng-baak mai jauh-dou.
- **b** _____ léuhng-gaan jauh-dou gaau-tóng.
- **c** Hei-yún hàahng-_____ géi-gāan jau-dou.
- **d** _____ léuhng-go jūng-tàuh jauh-dou fó-chē-jaahm.

Points: _____ /4

Total points: _____ /56

食乜嘢？ *Sihk-māt-yéh?*

What shall we eat?

In this unit you will learn how to:

▶ *request basic food and drinks.*
▶ *order food in a restaurant.*
▶ *express preferences.*

CEFR: (A2) *Can order a meal; can say what he/she wants; can say what he/she prefers.*

食在香港 Sihk-joih Hēung-góng
Eating out in Hong Kong

Eating is the most popular pastime among Hong Kongers. Indeed, it is appropriately described in a local saying, **màhn-yíh sihk-wàih-tīn** (*eating is heavenly*). An entrepreneurial spirit has made the regional cuisines of China a desirable commodity. You don't need to travel far to enjoy **Bǎk-gīng-choi** (*Beijing food*), **Seuhng-hói-choi** (*Shanghai food*), **Sei-cyūn-choi** (*Sichuan food*), **Chiuchow** food, **Hakka** food, and of course the spectacular varieties of **Gwóng-dūng-choi** (*Gwongdong food*).

For Westerners, such dishes as chickens' feet and duck tongue sound daunting. However, to acquaint oneself with Cantonese food culture, there is no harm trying such delicacies as beef congee, **wàhn-tān-mihn** (*won-ton noodles*), **chāa-sīu** (*barbecue pork*), and all kinds of **dím-sām** (*dim sum – small plates of snacks; literally touch the heart*). You might even grow passionate about them!

In most cases, however, the names of dishes are unlikely to signal what you are getting. You will therefore need to ask some useful questions, such as: **Nī-dihp[-choi]yáuh-mē-yéh haih-leuíh-minh aa?** (*What is in this dish?*); **Yáuh-móuh-yuhk hái-leuíh-mihn nē?** (*Does it contain meat?*); **Laaht-m̀h-laaht gaa?** (*Is it spicy?*); or **Ngóh-séung sihk-jāai** (*I want vegetarian food*).

 Find as many examples of the word **choi** as you can in the text and underline them. What do you think it means?

Vocabulary builder

07.01 Look at the following phrases, which are used in the dialogue. Note their meanings. Try pronouncing each word on your own. Now, listen to the audio and try to imitate the pronunciation of the speakers.

食物 *SIHK-MAHT* FOOD

頭盤 *Tàauh-pùhn* Starters

| 一碗雜菜湯 | yāt-wún jahp-choi tōng | *a bowl of mixed vegetable soup* |
| 一碟蝦片 | yāt-dihp hā-pín | *a plate of prawn crackers* |

主菜 *Jyū-choi* Main dishes

一碟白飯	yāt-dihp baahk-faahn	*a plate of boiled rice*
一碟/炒飯/ 炒麵	yāt-dihp cháau-faahn/ cháau-mihn	*a plate of fried rice/fried noodles*
一碟咖喱雞	yāt-dihp ga-lēi-gāi	*a plate of curried chicken*
一碟白菜	yāt-dihp baahk-choi	*a plate of Chinese cabbage*

> **LANGUAGE TIP**
>
> **Sā** and **wú** are kinds of porridge with different textures and density. In this text, both of them are translated as *soup*.

甜品 *Tìhm-bán* Desserts

一碗紅豆沙	yāt-wún hùhng-dáu-sā	*a bowl of red-bean soup*
一碗芝麻糊	yāt-wún jī-màh-wú	*a bowl of sesame soup*
一杯/啲雪糕	yāt-būi/dī syut-gōu	*a cup of ice cream/some ice cream*

飲品 *Yám-bán* Drinks

一支汽水	yāt-jī hei-séui	*a bottle of soft drink*
一杯紅/白/餐酒	yāt-būi hùhng-/baahk-/ cāan-jáu	*a glass of red/white/ table wine*
一杯啤酒	yāt-būi bē-jáu	*a glass of beer*
一杯咖啡/茶	yāt-būi ga-fēi/chàh	*a cup of coffee/tea*
一杯清水	yāt-būi chīng-séui	*a glass of (tap) water*

There are a number of classifiers such as **dihp** (*plate*) used in the list. Can you identify them? What are they?

生詞 *SĀANG-CHÌH* NEW EXPRESSIONS

想…啲咩呀？	Séung … -dī mē-aa?	*What do you want to/prefer … ?*
重想要…？	Juhng séung-yiu … ?	*in addition to … (literally still want)*
要唔要…呀？	yiu-m̀h-yiu … aa?	*(Do you) want … ? (literally want not want … ?)*

喺咁多？	Haih-gám dō?	Is that all?
喺咁多。	Haih-gám dō.	That's all.
食	sihk	eat
飲	yám	drink
俾個…	Béi go …	literally Give me a …
餐牌	chāan-páai	menu
…同埋…	… tùhng-máaih …	… and … (also in Unit 5)
唔該……添。	M̀h-gōi … tīm.	Please … also.
唔該埋單。	M̀h-gōi màaih-dāan.	The bill, please. (literally Close the bill.)

Conversation 1

07.02 *Wendy and Bob are in a Cantonese restaurant. The néuih-sih-ying (waitress) asks what they would like to have for dinner.*

1 Listen to the conversation. Who orders soup? What else does Wendy want?

Wendy	M̀h-gōi béi-go chāan-páai ngóh.
Néuih-si-ying	Hóu-aa, séung-sihk-mē nē?
Wendy	M̀h-gōi yāt-wún jaahp-choi-tōng, tùhng-màaih yāt-dihp cháau-faahn.
Néuih si-ying	(*Turning to Bob*) Sīn-sāang, néih-nē?
Bob	Yāt-dihp hā-pín, yāt-dihp chā-sīu, tùhng-màaih yāt-dihp cháau-mihn.
Néuih si-ying	Hóu-aa, séung-yám-dī mē nē?
Bob	Yāt-jī huhng-jáu. Ngóh juhng-séung-yiu-dī chīng-séui tīm.
Néuih si-ying	Gám yiu-m̀h-yiu tìhm-bán aa?
Wendy	Gám-àah, ngóh-yiu-būi jī-màh syut-gōu.
Bob	Gám ngóh-yiu wún hùhng-dáu-sā lāa. M̀h-gōi léuhng-būi ga-fē tīm.
Néuih si-ying	Haih-gam-dō?
Bob	Haih-aa, hái-gam-dō.
	At the end of the dinner …
Bob	M̀h-gōi màaih-dāan.

> **PRONUNCIATION**
> Note the tone difference between **gám** (*so/then*) as in **gám-àah** (*is that so*), and **gam** (*such/so*) as in **Haih-gam-dō?/!** (*Is that all?/That's all!*)

> **LANGUAGE TIP**
> **yiu-būi/wún** … (*like to have a cup/bowl of* …) is short for **yiu-yāt-būi/wún** … (*like to have one cup/bowl of* …). **Yāt-būi/wún** … (*one cup/bowl of* …) is usually preceded by *please, thank you, excuse me*, etc.

2 **Match the Chinese and the English.**

a   Ṁh-gōi yāt-wún jaahp-choi-tōng.   **1**   The bill, please.

b   Séung-yám-dī mē-nē?   **2**   Would you like a dessert?

c   Ngóh junhg-séung-yiu-dī   **3**   A bowl of vegetable soup,
    chīn-séui tīm.   please.

d   Ngoh-yiu-būi jī-màh   **4**   I would also like some tap
    syut-gōu?   water.

e   Néih yiu-ṁh-yiu tìhm-bán nē?   **5**   What would you like to drink?

f   Ṁh-gōi màaih-dāan.   **6**   I would like some sesame
                                                   ice cream.

3 **Read the conversation and answer the questions.**

a   What does Bob order?

b   Do they order red or white wine?

c   What is Wendy having for dessert?

4 07.03 **Now listen to the lines from the conversation and repeat.
Then listen to the waiter's lines and Bob's lines and answer as if
you were Wendy.**

💡 Language discovery 1

1 **Look at Conversation 1 again. What is the Cantonese for these
phrases?**

a   Could you please let me have the menu?

b   What do you want to drink?

c   In addition, I would like to have some water.

俾…我 *BÉI . . . NGÓH* GIVE ME . . .

This is a convenient word for requesting something as in **béi-go chāan-
páai ngóh** (*let me have the menu*), **béi-jī-jáu ngóh** (*let me have a bottle
of wine*). It is usually followed by a classifier such as **go, jī, dihp** etc. And
ngóh is put at the end of the sentence.

2 **Translate the following into Cantonese.**

a   Please let me have the menu.

b   Please let me have a bottle of water.

想…咩呀? *SÉUNG . . . MĒ-NĒ?* WHAT . . . DO YOU WANT?

This is a useful expression for asking about preferences. One can always say
Sihk-dī mē-nē? (literally *Eat what?*); **Yám-dī mē-nē?** (literally *Drink what?*).
If one speaks quickly and loudly, one can sound very rude. To soften the

tone, we precede the question with **séung** (literally *want*, *hope*) as in **Séung sihk-dī mē-nē?** *What would you like to eat?* (literally *Want eat anything?*).

3 Can you now give the Cantonese for *What would you like to drink?*

仲想…*JUHNG-SÉUNG* . . . IN ADDITION, I WOULD LIKE . . .

This is another commonly used expression to express the idea that one wants something more than what has already been said. It goes with almost all kinds of verbs as in **juhng-séung sihk-faahn** (literally *still want to eat rice*); **juhng-séung yám-jáu** (literally *still want to drink wine*). So, **Ngóh juhng-séung yiu cháau-faahn** is *In addition, I would like to have some fried rice*.

4 Give the Cantonese for *In addition, I would like to have a cup of coffee*.

> **DON'T FORGET**
> Adding **deih** turns singular pronouns into plurals (see Unit 1), as in **ngóh** (*I, me*): **ngóh-deih** (*we, us*); **néih** (*you*: singular): **néih-deih** (*you*: plural); **kéuih** (*he, she,* or *it*): **kéuih-dēi** (*they, them*).

5 Translate these sentences into Cantonese and read them out loud.
  a We want two sparkling waters.
  b They prefer wine.

REQUESTS

To request something politely in Cantonese, we can use the following expressions:

Deui-m̀h-jyuh, ngóh-séung-yiu . . . as in **Deui-m̀h-jyuh, ngóh-séung-yiu-go chāan-pāai.** (literally *Excuse me, I would like to have the menu*.)

M̀h-gōi, ngóh-séung-yiu . . . as in **M̀h-gōi, ngóh-séung-yiu-dihp chā-sīu.** (literally *Thank you, I would like to have barbecue pork*.)

M̀h-gōi-néih hó-m̀h-hó-yíh . . . as in **M̀h-gōi-néih hó-m̀h-hó-yíh béi-būi ga-fē ngóh.** (literally *Thank you, may I have a cup of coffee?*)

Practice 1

1 Translate the following into Cantonese.

  a Could we have some tap water?

  b Can I have the bill, please?

  c I prefer fried noodles.

  d I would like to have some sesame ice cream.

2 Complete the following sentences with the appropriate expressions to form polite requests.

  a _____, néih-séung sihk-dī-mē nē?

  b _____ màaih-dāan.

  c _____, ngóh-sēung yiu-jī-hùhng-jáu.

  d _____ béi-būi chīng-séui-ngóh.

3 Fill in the appropriate classifiers.

  a Kéuih-yiu _____ húng-jāu.

  b M̀h-gōi béi _____ cháau-faahn ngóh-lāa.

  c Yāt-_____ hèih-séui, m̀h-gōi.

  d Ngóh-séung-yiu _____ hùhng-dauh-sā.

 4 You are dining out with a friend. Follow the prompts and place your order.

You	*Could I have a menu please?*
Néuih sih-ying	Hóu-aa, séung-sihk-mē nē?
You	*We would like to have two bowls of vegetable soup.*
Néuih sih-ying	Hóu-aa, séung-yám-dī-mé nē?
You	*We would like to have a bottle of red wine. In addition, I would like to have some ice cream.*

 Listen and understand

1 07.04 **Listen and circle what Joey is ordering from the Gām-yāt jīng-syún (Today's menu).**

> ### Today's Menu
>
> mixed vegetable soup   fried noodle   Chinese cabbage   ice cream
> prawn crackers   seafood fried noodle   red-bean soup   soft drink
> fried rice   curry chicken   sesame soup   tea

2 07.05 **What kind of drinks do Alfred and Fion have with their meal? Listen carefully to their conversation with the sih-ying-sān (waiter) and fill in the gaps. Listen again, and imitate the pronunciation of the speakers.**

Sih-ying-sāng	Néih-deih séung-sihk-dī-mē nē?
Alfred	Ngóh-séung yiu-jī _____.
Sih-ying-sāng	Baahk-jáu dihng hùhng-jáu nē?
Alfred	Ngóh-yiu-būi _____, m̀h-gōi.
Fion	Ngóh-yiu-būi _____.

> **DON'T FORGET**
> **Dihng** is short for
> **dihng-haih** (or; literally
> *unalterably is*).

3 07.06 **Listen to the requests you hear. Then indicate whether they are F (formal) or I (informal).**
 a Chéng-mahn-néih séung-sihk-dī mē-nē?
 b Yám-dī mē-nē?
 c Màaih-dāan!
 d M̀h-gōi màaih-dāan.

 4 07.07 **Listen to the pronunciation of hái** (at, in, on) **and haih** (be), and try to imitate the speakers.

Sih-ying-sāng	Nī haih-m̀h-haih séung-giu cháau-faahn aa?
You	Yáuh-móuh-yuhk hái-leúih-mihn nē?
Sih-ying-sāng	Cháau-faahn leúih-mihn haih-yáuh-gāi, yáuh-hā, tùhng-máaih yáuh-choi.
You	Chéng-mahn sái-sáu-gāan hái-bīn-douh nē?
Sih-ying-sāng	Hái-néih jó-mihn. (see Unit 6)

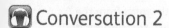

Conversation 2

07.08 *Aslan, Josephine, and Kam-leung, Aslan's brother, are stopping in a café for a snack. The waitress (Néuih-sih-ying) takes the order. Listen and answer the question.*

1   Which of the three friends order a sandwich?

Néuih-sih-ying	Hāaa-lóu, ngh-ōn. Chéng-mahn néih-deih séung-yiu-dī-mē nē?
Aslan	(*Turning to Josephine*) Josephine, néih-séung yām-dī-mē nē?
Josephine	Ngóh-séung yiu-būi cháang-jāp.
Aslan	Séung-sihk-dī-mē nē?
Josephine	Fó-téui sāam-màhn-jih laa.
Aslan	(*Turning to Kam-leung*) Néih-nē, gòh-gō? Séung-sihk-dī-mē aa?
Kam-leung	Ngóh àah? ga-fē-gā-náaih, tùhng-màaih jī-sí sāam-màhn-jih laa.
Néuih-sih-ying	Gám néih-nē, sīn-sāang?
Aslan	Ngóh-yiu pìhng-gwo-jāp tùhng-màaih fó-téui-sā-lēut.
Néuih-sih-ying	Juhng-yiu-dī-mē.nē?
Aslan	M̀h-gōi béi-būi-chīng-séui-ngóh tīm.

> **PRONUNCIATION**
> Note the tone difference in the question words **aa** (used in neutral questions) and **àah** (expecting agreement).

V More words!

ngh-on	*good afternoon*
Chéng-mahn?	literally *May I ask?*
yám	*drink*
fó-téui sāam-màhn-jih	*ham sandwich*
ga-fē-gā-náih	*white coffee* (literally *coffee with milk*)
jī-síh sāam-màhn-jih	*cheese sandwich*
sā-lēut	*salad*
cháang/pìhng-gwó-jāp	*orange/apple juice*

2 **Complete the Cantonese expressions with words from the conversation. Then only look at the English translations and test yourself.**

a yāt-dihp _____   *a plate of salad*
b yāt-būi _____   *an orange juice*
c _____ gā-náaih   *coffee with milk*
d fó téui _____   *ham sandwich*
e _____ sāam-màhn-jih   *cheese sandwich*
f píhng-gwo _____   *apple juice*
g yāt-būi _____   *a glass of water*

3 **Listen to the conversation again, then answer these questions.**
   a What is Kam-leung having?
   b What is Aslan drinking?
   c What else does Aslan order?

 ## Language discovery 2

There are three phrases used in the conversation indicating *What do you want to have?* What are they?

In Cantonese, there are many ways of asking people what they are going to have. For example:

Néih-séung yiu-dī mē nē?   literally *What do you want to have?*
Néih-séung giu-dī mē nē?   literally *What do you want to order?*
Néih-séung sihk-dī mē nē?   literally *What do you want to eat?*
Néih-séung yám-dī mē nē?   literally *What do you want to drink?*

Dím-sám (*dim sum*) is a significant feature of Cantonese food (much like Spanish tapas). Cantonese people have it mainly for breakfast or lunch. The **chàh-làuh** (*tea house*) serves both tea and a range of dim sum, which are traditionally placed on a trolley for customers to see and select. Tea and dim sum are often inseparable. For this reason, when inviting friends to come along for dim sum, Cantonese people say **heui-yám-chàh** (literally *let's go drinking tea*).

The term **cháh-làuh** (*tea house*) is a traditional but casual alternative to **jáu-làuh/jáu-gā** (*restaurants*), which are more commonly used nowadays. Some useful terms are:

中國茶 *JŪNG-GWOK-CHÀH* POPULAR CHINESE TEAS

一壺香片	**yāt-wùh hēung-pín**	*a pot of Jasmine tea (light)*
一壺普洱	**yāt-wùh póu-léi/bóu-léi**	*a pot of pu'er tea (black)*
一壺水仙	**yāt-wùh séui-sīn**	*a pot of narcissus tea (light)*

點心 *DIM-SAM* POPULAR DIM SUM

一籠蝦餃	**yāt-lùhng hā-gáau**	*a basket of shrimp dumplings*
一籠燒買	**yāt-lùhng sīu-máai**	*a basket of pork and shrimp dumplings*
一碟春卷	**yāt-dihp chēun-gyún**	*a plate of spring rolls*

Practice 2

1 Complete the following with the appropriate word.

   a Néih-séung _____ dī-mē nē? (*eat*)

   b Néih-séung _____ dī-mē nē? (*have*)

   c Néih-séung _____ dī-mē nē? (*drink*)

2 Re-arrange the sentences below to form a dialogue.

   ___ Juhng-séung yiu dī-mē nē?

   ___ Ngóh-séung yiu-wùh bóu-léi.

   ___ Ngóh juhng-séung yiu-dip chēun-gyún.

   ___ Chéng-mahn néih-séung giu-dī mē-nē?

> **PRONUNCIATION**
> **Bóu-léi** (*pu'er tea*) is a more common pronunciation than **póu-léi**.

Speaking

You and a friend go into a **chàh-chāan-tēng** (*Chinese-style café*) for a drink and a snack. The **fó-gei** (*waiter*) is ready to take your order.

Fó-gei	Néih-deih séung sīhk-dī mē-nē?
You	*A glass of apple juice, a chicken sandwich, and a black coffee for my friend.*
Fó-gei	Néih-nē?
You	*I would like to have a glass of water, a hamburger, and a white coffee.*

V More words!

gāi-yuhk sāam-màhn-jih	*chicken sandwich*
ga-fē jáu-náaih	*black coffee* (literally *coffee running away from milk*)
hon-bóu-bāau	*hamburger*

Fó-gei is a traditional term for *waiter* or *waitress*. Like many Cantonese words, **fó-gei** has evolved to be used in less prestigious outlets such as **chàh-chāan-tēng** (*Chinese-style café*) and **daaih-pàih-dong** (*open food stall*).

Reading and writing

You are hungry. When you pass a **chàh-chāan-tēng**, a menu is placed near the door. Read it carefully. Use the information in the Vocabulary builder to help you.

是日供應 SIH-YAHT GŪNG-YING
Today's Menu

一人套餐 Yāt-yàhn-tou-cāan Set Menu for One	二人套餐 Yih-yàhn-tou-cāan Set Menu for Two
雜菜湯 雞炒飯 紅豆沙 香片茶	春卷 咖喱雞 白菜 白飯 芝麻糊 汽水
(十元 sahp-yùhn $10)	(十六元 sahp-luk-yùhn $16)

---

1 **Answer the following questions.**
   a What does 'Set menu for one' consist of?
   b What are the food and drink only offered in 'Set menu for two'?

2 **Try writing in Chinese characters: $10 and $16.**

Test yourself

1 Read the following and spot the odd one out in each line.

a chāa-siu, hùhng-dáu-sā, jī-màh-wú, syut-gōu

b bē-jáu, chīng-séui, ga-lēi-gāi, pìhng-gwo-jāp

c hāh-gáau, sīu-máaih, chēun-gyún, gūk-fā

2 07.09 **What are Theo and Kaia having to drink and to eat? Listen and make a note.**

8

平日做咩呢？
Pìhng-yaht jouh mē nē?
What are your daily activities?

In this unit you will learn how to:
▶ *talk about your regular activities.*
▶ *say how often you do certain things.*
▶ *indicate when places open and close.*

CEFR (A2): *Can give a simple description of daily routine; can ask and answer questions about habits and routines; can ask and answer questions about what we do in our free time.*

工作狂 Gūng-jok-kòhng *Workaholics*

It's all too easy to see Hong Kongers as workaholics – they eat fast, talk fast, walk fast, have more than one job, and stay at their **baahn-gūng-sāt** (*offices*) way beyond five o'clock in the evening. While the high cost of living is a factor, the strong work ethic also plays an important role. In theory, the working day in **jing-fú bouh-mùhn** (*government offices*) starts at nine and finishes at around five, with an hour's **ńgh-sihn** (*lunch break*). Shop **hōi-mùhn sìh-gan** (*opening times*) vary, and many will not **sāan-mùhn** (*close*) during lunchtime. **Ngàhn-hòhng** (*banks*), however, are normally open from nine to four.

To ask about the opening and closing times of, for example, a library, one can say: **[Tòuh-syū-gún] géi-dím hōi-mùhn aa?** (*What time does [the library] open?*); **Géi-dím sāan-mùhn nē?** (*What time does [it] close?*) Although the city is not too big, people leave early for work to avoid traffic jams, usually **sihk ngaan-jau** (*have lunch*) nearby, and get back home **sihk máahn-faahn** (*for supper*).

 What is the Cantonese for *lunch* and *supper*? Find the words in the text, and underline them.

Vocabulary builder

 08.01 **Look at the following phrases and complete the missing English. Note their meanings. Try pronouncing each word on your own. Now listen to the audio and imitate the sounds as closely as you can.**

日常起居 *YAHT-SÈUHNG HÉI-GĒUI* DAILY ROUTINE

返工	fāan-gūng	*go to work*
放工	fōng-gūng	*finish _____*
起身	héi-sān	*get _____; literally up-body*
沖涼	chūng-lèuhng	*have a wash (an umbrella term for taking a shower or bath)*
擦牙	chaat-ngàh	*brush teeth*
洗面	sái-mihn	*wash face*
食早餐	sihk jóu-chāan	*have breakfast*
瞓覺	fan-gaau	*go to sleep*

消遣 *SĪU-HÍN* LEISURE TIME

去睇戲	heui tái-hei	*literally go to watch a movie*
去健身室	heui gihn-sān-sāt	*_____ the gym*
做運動	jouh-wahn-duhng	*do exercises*
打網球	dáai-móhng-kàuh	*_____ tennis*
睇電視/報紙	tái-dihn-sih/bou-jí	*watch television/read a newspaper*
聽音樂	tēng-yām-ngohk	*_____ to music*
上網	séuhng-mòhng	*surf the internet*

生詞 *SĀANG-CHÌH* NEW EXPRESSIONS

點樣…?	Dím-yéung…?	*How do you…?*
咁喺邊度…?	Gám hái-bīn-douh…?	*Where do you…?*
做啲咩呢?	Jouh-dī-mē nē?	*What do you do?*
至	ji	*till*
完	yùhn	*finish*
之後	jī-hauh	*after*
通常	tūng-sèuhng	*usually*
時時	sìh-sìh	*always*
然後	yìhn-hauh	*then*
行路	hàahng-louh	*walk*
同啲同事	tùhng-dī tùhng-sih	*with my colleagues*
喺附近	hái fuh-gahn	*nearby*
快餐店	faai-chāan-dim	*fast-food restaurant*
返屋企	fāan ūk-kéi	*go home*
有時去…	yáuh-sìh-heui…	*sometimes go to…*
好早瞓	hóu-jóu fan	*sleep very early (literally very early sleep)*
好夜瞓	hóu-yeh fan	*sleep very late (literally very late sleep)*

PARTICLES introduced in this unit

喍	gaa	*final particle indicating emphasis or surprise*

Conversation 1

08.02 *Billy tells Winnie, a colleague, about his day.*

1 Listen and answer the question. What are Billy's working hours?

Winnie	Néih géi-dím fāan-gūng, géi-dím fong-gūng gaa?
Billy	Ngóh gáu-dím fāan-gūng, luhk-dím fong-gūng.
Winnie	Géi-dím héi-sān nē?
Billy	Ngóh chāt-dím héi-sān chūng-lèuhng, chaat-ngàh, sái-mihn, sihk jóu-chāan, yìhn-hauh fāan-gūng.
Winnie	Néih dím-yéung fāan-gūng gaa? Hàahng-louh dihng-haih daap bā-sí nē?
Billy	Ngóh sìh-sìh-doū daap bā-sí.
Winnie	Gám hái bīn-douh sihk ngaan-jau nē?
Billy	Tùhng-dī tùhng-sih hái fuh-gahn gāan fai-chāan-dim sihk- ngaan-jau.
Winnie	Néih fong-gūng jī-hauh tūng-seuhng jouh-dī-mē nē?
Billy	Ngóh tūng fāan-ūk-kéi. Yáuh-sìh heui dá móhng-kàuh, yáuh-sìh héui-gym, yáuh-sìh heui tái-hei.
Winnie	Néih haih-m̀h-haih hóu-jóu-fan gaa?
Billy	M̀h-haih wo, ngóh hóu-yeh-jí-fan gaa. Sihk-yùhn máahn-faahn-jī-haauh, jauh tái bou-jí, séuhng-móhng, waahk-jé tái dihn-sih.

> **LANGUAGE TIP**
> **Sihk-fahn** (literally *eat rice*) is an umbrella term for **sihk-ngaan-jau** (*have lunch*) and **sihk-máahn-fahn** (*have supper*).

V **jī-haauh** (*after*); **jauh** (*right away, forthwith*); **waahk-jé** (*perhaps*)

2 Match the Cantonese with the English.

a Ngóh daap-bā-sí.	**1** I read the newspaper.
b Ngóh-hái faai-chāan-dim sihk ngaan-jau.	**2** I go to the gym.
c Ngóh fāan-ūk-kéi.	**3** I watch TV.
d Ngóh heui-gihn-sán-sát.	**4** I go on the bus.
e Ngóh tái-dihn-sih.	**5** I have lunch in a fast-food restaurant.
f Ngóh tái-bou-jí.	**6** I come back home.

3 Read or listen to the conversation again, then answer the questions.
  a What time does Billy usually get up?
  b What does he do after he gets up?
  c What does he do when he finishes work?
  d What does he do before he goes to bed?

4 08.03 **Now listen to the lines from the conversation and repeat. Then listen to Winnie's lines and reply as if you were Billy.**

1 Which expression has the same meaning as *how* in English?

點樣? *DÍM-YÉUNG*? HOW?

In Unit 4, we learned to use the phrase **géi-dím** (*what time*) to check the time of day. To ask *how*, we use the expression **dím-yéung** as in:

Néih dím-yéung fáan-gūng gaa?
How do you get to work? (literally *You how go work* + final particle)

Néih dím-yéung heui-faai-chāan-dim gaa?
How do you get to the fast-food restaurant?
(literally *You how go fast-food restaurant* +
final particle)

> **LANGUAGE TIP**
> In the examples shown, **gaa** can be replaced with other such final particles as **nē** and **aa** depending on the message needing to be expressed.

Néih dim-yéung heui-gihn-sān-sāt gaa?
How do you get to the gym? (literally *You how go gym* + final particle)

搭乜嘢? *DAAP-MĀT-YÉH ...?* HOW DO YOU GET TO ...?

Another way of asking *how* is to use **māt-yéh** and restructure the sentence as follows:

Néih daap-māt-yéh fāan-gūng gaa?
How do you get to work?

Néih daap-māt-yéh heui-faai-chāan-dim gaa?
How do you get to the fast-food restaurant?

Néih daap-māt-yéh heui gihn-sān-sāt gaa?
How do you get to the gym?

You can answer those questions by saying **Ngóh daap ...** (*I take ...*) as in:

Ngóh daap-bā-sí fāan-gūng.
I take the bus to work.

Ngóh daap dihn-chē heui faai-chāan-dim.
I take the tram to the fast-food restaurant.

Ngo daap dei-tit heui gihn-sān-sāt.
I take the MTR to the gym.

2 Read Conversation 1 again. Can you find the expressions that mean *always*, *usually*, and *sometimes*? Write them down and say them out loud.

HOW OFFEN

 08.04 **To say how often you do certain things you can use:**

sìh-sìh; gīng-sèuhng	*always*
pìhng-yāt	*normally* (literally *on normal days*)
tūng-sèuhng	*usually*
gaan-m̀h-jūng; yáuh-sìh	*sometimes*
chùhng-lòih m̀h-wúih	*never* (literally *never would*)

Practice 1

1 **Match the Cantonese phrases with the appropriate English phrases.**

a	sihk jóu-chāan	**1**	take a shower
b	tái-bou-jī	**2**	surf the net
c	séuhng-móhng	**3**	have breakfast
d	chūng-lèuhng	**4**	read the newspaper

2 **Complete the following sentences with the appropriate verbs.**

tēng	**jouh**	**dá**	**tái**

a Fohng-jou gūng jī-hauh, ngóh jeui jūng-yi _____ dihn-sih.
b Sīng-kèih-yāt, ngóh heui _____ -móhng-kàuh.
c Sihk-yùhn-faahn-hauh, ngóh jauh _____ yām-ngohk.
d Sīng-kèih-luhk, ngóh heui _____ wahn-duhng.

> **LANGUAGE TIP**
> **jeui jūng-yi** literally *most like*

3 **Answer the following questions about yourself.**
   a Néih géi-dím héi-sān aa?
   b Néih géi-dím fāan-gūng nē?
   c Néih dím-yéung fāan-gūng gaa?
   d Néih géi-dím fong-gūng nē?

🎧 Listen and understand

1 08.05 **Siu-ping asks Kam-chung, a university student, what his typical day is like. Listen and complete Kam-chung's schedule.**

> 7.30 héi-sān
> 8.30 _____
> 1.00 hái daaih-hohk go-douh _____
> 5.00 _____
> 7.00 sihk máahn-faahn

> **LANGUAGE TIP**
> **séuhng-chòhng** (*go to bed*); **fan-gaau** is the extended form of **fan** (*sleep*)

2 08.06 **How often do Chi-wai and Suk-yi do each of the following? Listen and choose the appropriate expression.**

| sìh-sìh | tūng-seung | gaan-nh-jūng |
| chùhng-lòih-nh-wui | pìhng-yàt | |

> **LANGUAGE TIP**
> **hóu-yeh** (*very late at night*; literally *very 'nightful'*)

a Kéuih-deih ^6.45 héi-sān.
b Kéuih-deih ^8.00 heui-fāan-gūng.
c Kéuih-deih ^daap déih-tit.
d Kéuih-deih ^6.00 fong-gūng.
e Kéuih-deih^ hóu yeh-fan.

3 08.07 **Native Cantonese speakers tend to use short forms, giving the impression that they speak fast. You do not need to imitate their speed when you speak, but it would be good if you could get used to their 'shortened' speech.**

Listen to the following phrases. When you feel confident, take up the challenge and imitate the 'shortened' speech of the speakers.

a Néih géi-dím fāan-gūng aa? (short for Néih géi-dō dím fāan-gūng aa?)
b Yáuh-sìh heui dá-móhng kàuh. (short for Yáuh sìh-haauh heui dá móhng kàuh.)
c Néih fong-gūng jī-hauh jouh-dī mē nē? (short for Néih fong-gūng jī-hauh jouh-dī māt-yéh nē?)
d Néih Sīng-kèi-luhk jouh-mē nē? (short for Néih Sīng-kèi-luhk jouh-dī mē nē?)
e Gám hái-bīn aa? (short for Gám-hái bīn-douh aa?)

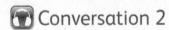 Conversation 2

08.08 Listen to Roland asking Pui-fan what she and her husband do at weekends.

1 Do Pui-fan and Edmund get up early on Saturdays?

Roland	Pui-fān, néih-tùhng Edmund Sīng-kèih-luhk-yaht jouh-dī-mē nē?
Pui-fan	Sīng-kèih-luhk, ngóh-deih hóu-ngaan-ji héi-sān gaa. Edmund heui gihn-sān-sāt. Ngóh heui dá-móhng-kàuh.
Roland	Pìhng-yāt bīn-go jyú-faahn nē?
Pui-fan	Tūng-sèuhng haih-ngóh.
Roland	Gám néih-deih ngaan-jau jouh-dī-mē nē?
Pui-fan	Edmund wui tái-bou-jí. Ngóh yáuh-sìh séuhng-móhng, yáuh-sìh tēng-yām-ngohk.
Roland	Gám néih-deih Sing-kèih-yāt jouh-dī mē-nē?
Pui-fan	Sīng-kèih-yāt ngóh-deih tūng-sèuhng heui hàahng-sāan.

 hóu-ngaan (*very late in the day*; literally *very 'dayful'*); **páau-bouh** (*jogging*); **jyú-faahn** (*cook*); **hàahng-sāan** (*hiking*); **dōu-wui** (*also*)

2 Match the Cantonese phrases with the English.

a	dá móhng-kàuh	**1**	to cook
b	hàahng-sāan	**2**	to go jogging
c	jyú-faahn	**3**	to play tennis
d	páau-bouh	**4**	to go hiking

3 Read or listen to the conversation again and decide if the following statements are T (true) or F (false).

a On Saturday morning Edmund goes out jogging and Pui-fan listens to music.

b Edmund always does the cooking.

c In the afternoon Pui-fan takes a nap.

d On Saturday night they go dancing with friends.

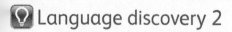
Language discovery 2

1 **Read Conversation 2 again. Can you find the Cantonese equivalents of the following expressions:**

   a We get up very late on Saturday.
   b Who normally does the cooking?
   c Edmund reads the newspaper.

邊個? *BĪN-GO?* WHO?

When asking who is responsible for doing what, we use the expression **bīn-go** in Cantonese, as in **Bīn-go jyú-faahn nē?** (*Who cooks?*), and **Bīn-go yáuh-sìh heui hàahng-sāan nē?** (*Who sometimes goes hiking?*). The particle **nē** is at the end of the statement to make it a question. However, you can still turn such a statement into a question by raising the tone of the last word (as you would do in English).

2 **Now, try to give the Cantonese equivalents for the following:**

   a Who listens to music?
   b Who normally surfs the net?

至 *JI* TILL

The literal meaning of **ji** is *till*, but it can be regarded as the equivalent of English *not till*. At the moment, however, we will confine the use of **ji** to *lateness*, as in **Ngóh hóu-ngaan ji héi-sān** (*I don't get up till late*); **Kéuih hóu-ngaan ji fāan-gūng** (*He/she doesn't go to work till late*); and **Kéuih-deih hóu-yeh ji fan-gaau** (*They go to bed very late*).

3 **Translate the following sentences into Cantonese.**

   a He doesn't come home till late.
   b She doesn't cook till late.

🏛 *WUÍH* SHALL/WILL

Wuíh has multiple meanings. In this context, like the English *shall/will*, **wuíh** serves to predict things that are likely to happen. So *He will read the newspaper* is **Kéuih wuíh tái-bou-jí**. *She will listen to music* is **Kéuih wuíh tēng-yām-ngohk**. **Wuíh** can also be used before the verb **yáuh** (*have*), as in **Gāam-máahn wuíh-yáuh faahn-sihk**, literally *Tonight there will be a meal to eat*.

4 **Can you translate the following sentences into Cantonese?**

    a They will go hiking.
    b They will play tennis.

 Practice 2

1 **Complete the following sentences with the right word.**

bīn-go	ji	wui

    a Sīng-kèih-luhk néih _____ jouh mē-nē?
    b Kéuih-deih hóu ngaan _____ hēi-sān.
    c Pìhng-yāt _____ jyú-faahn nē?
    d Kéuih sìh-sìh hóu-yeh _____ fāan ūk-kéi.

2 **Talk to Ga-hou, and see what he and Barbara, his wife, do on Saturdays. Ask the questions in Cantonese.**

You	*Ga-hou, what do you and Barbara do on Saturdays?*
Ga-hou	Sīng-kèih-luhk ngóh deih hóu-ngāan ji hēi-sān gaa.
You	*Who normally cooks?*
Ga-hou	Tūng-sèuhng haih-ngóh.
You	*So what do you normally do in the afternoon?*
Ga-hou	Barbara wui tēng-yām-ngohk. Ngóh yáuh-sìh séuhng-móhng, yáuh-sìh tái-bou-jí.

Reading and writing

Wai-sam (慧心) is a cartoonist. In order to attract customers, she has created a blog. On it, she illustrates her daily activities with some cartoons.

1 **Match the following three expressions with Wai-sam's cartoons by filling out the blanks either with a, b, c, or if you are confident enough, the Chinese characters.**

 a 漫畫家／漫画家 (cartoonist)
 b 聽音樂／听音乐 (listen to music)
 c 行街睇戲／行街睇戏 (go shopping and watching movies)

我叫慧心，係個＿＿＿＿＿＿＿＿。
我叫慧心，係个＿＿＿＿＿＿＿＿。
Ngóh gīu Wai-sam. Haih go maahn-wá-gā.

我日日七點半起身，沖涼，擦牙，食早餐。
我日日七点半起身，冲凉，擦牙，食早餐。
Ngóh yaht-yaht chāt-dim bun hēi-sān, chūng-lèuhng, chāat-aa, sihk jóu-chāan.

我行路返工。
Ngóh hàahng-louh fāan-gūng.

2 **How much have you understood?**
 a When does Wai-sam get up?
 b How does Wai-sam get to work?
 c Apart from listening to music, what does she sometimes do in her leisure time?

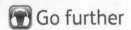 Go further

08.09 Listen and study these phrases related to opening and closing hours.

Bōk-maht-gún gēi-dím hōi-mùhn nē?	*What time does the museum open?*
Chīu-kāp-síh-chèuhng gēi-dím hōi-mùhn nē?	*What time do the supermarkets open?*
Ga-fē-sāt gēi-dim hōi-mùhm nē?	*What time does the café close?*
Jáu-bā gēi-dím sāan-mùhm nē?	*What time do the bars close?*
Hōi-jóu-mùhm laa!	*It's open!*
Sāan-jóu mùhm laa!	*It's closed!*

Test yourself

1   **Complete the sentences with the correct form of the verbs in brackets.**

sihk	héi	yám	fāan	séuhng
tái	fong	sihk	chūng	

a Ngóh bāat-dím-jūng _____gūng, ńgh-dím-jūng _____gūng.
b Ngóh chāt-dím _____sān, _____-lèuhng, _____-ga-fē.
c Ngóh sīn-sāan Gā-fai tùhng ngóh sìh-sìh hái ūk-kéi _____ngaan-jau.
d _____-yùhn-faahn haauh, ngóh jūng-yi _____-móhng tùhng-màaih _____dihn-sih.

2   08.10 **Listen to aa-Wing explaining what he, his wife aa-Sam, and their children do on Saturdays, then answer the questions.**

a What time do they get up?
b What do they do after breakfast?
c Who does the cooking?
d Where do aa-Wing and aa-Sam sometimes go in the evening?

SELF CHECK

	I CAN . . .
○	. . . talk about my regular activities.
○	. . . say how often I do certain things.
○	. . . indicate when places open and close.

9

噚日做咗乜？
Chàhm-yaht jouh-jó māt?

What did you do yesterday?

In this unit you will learn how to:
▶ *talk about past events.*
▶ *say what you like or dislike.*
▶ *give biographical information.*

CEFR (A2): *Can ask and answer questions about pastimes, past activities and personal experiences; can say what he/she likes or dislikes.*

喜好　Héi-hou　*Hobbies*

The main sport in Hong Kong has traditionally been football, a British influence going as far back as the late 19th century. Other popular sports that attract both participants and spectators are basketball, badminton, table tennis, cycling, running, and **yàuh-séui** (*swimming*). On the one hand, rugby, another inheritance from the British, is still honoured in the city, on the other, **lùhng-jàu ging-douh** (*traditional dragon boat racing*) has an impact internationally. One extremely popular sport in the territory is **choi-máh** (*horse racing*), which brings in over 11 per cent of Hong Kong's tax revenue.

Watching sports, **dihn-sih kehk** (*soap operas*), and **sān-mán** (*news*) on television are things everyone would do in their leisure time. Mahjong, however, is the city's favourite pastime. To most Hong Kongers, Tai-chi chuan and calligraphy are national cultural treasures. But increasing numbers of young people also enjoy surfing the Internet and playing with electronic games.

If you are asked **Jāu-muht néih jouh-jó-dī-mē aa?** (*What did you do at the weekend?*), you might answer **Ngóh heui-jó tái-choi-máh** (*I went to see the horse racing*), or **Ngóh hái gūng-yún sá tai-gihk** (*I did tai-chi in the park*), or **Ngóh hái-ūk-kéi sé syū-faat** (*I practised calligraphy*).

There are two Cantonese words meaning *competition* in the text. Can you find them?

> **LANGUAGE TIP**
>
> **Màh-jéuk** (*mahjong*, literally *play sparrows*) is similar to the Western card game rummy. Like feng-shui (see Unit 5) and dim sum (see Unit 7), both mahjong and tai-chi are 'international spellings', which do not reflect the actual sounds of Cantonese. The Yale romanization used in this book has a different spelling system, but provides a more accurate guide for Cantonese pronunciation. Look out for other examples such as proper names.

Vocabulary builder

09.01 **Look at the words and phrases and complete the missing English expressions. Then listen to the words and try to imitate the speaker.**

娛樂 *YÙH-LOHK* ENTERTAINMENT

行公司	hàahng-gūng-sī	*go window shopping*
去旅行	heui-léuih-hàhng	*go travelling*
睇戲	heui-tái-hei	*go watching* _____
夜蒲	yeh-pòuh	*go clubbing*

運動 *WAHN-DUHNG* SPORTS

踢足球	tek-jūk-kàuh	*play* _____ (literally *kick football*)
打欖球	dá-láam-kàuh	*play rugby* (literally *hit rugby*)
打籃球	dá-làahm-kàuh	*play basketball* (literally *hit basketball*)
打羽毛球	dá-yúh-móuh-kàuh	*play badminton* (literally *hit badminton*)
打兵乓球	dá-bīng-pōng-bō	*play table tennis* (literally *hit table tennis*)
踩單車	cháai-dāan-chē	_____ (literally *step bicycles*)
滑雪	waaht-syut	*skiing*

生詞 *SĀANG-CHÌH* NEW EXPRESSIONS

做咩呀?	Jouh-mē aa?	*What do you do?* (literally *do what?*)
好唔好...呀?	...hóu-m̀h-hóu ... aa?	*Is it good?* (literally *good-not-good*)
鍾唔鍾意...呀?	...jūng-m̀h-jūng-yi ... aa?	*Do you like?* (literally *like-not-like*)
周末	jāu-muht	*weekend*
星期六日	Sīng-kèih-luhk-yaht	*Saturday and Sunday*
琴日/噚日	kàhm-yaht/chàhm-yaht	*yesterday* (see Unit 4)
朝頭早	jīu-tàuh-jóu	*morning*
下晝	hah-jau	*afternoon* (see Unit 4)
無出街	móuh chēut-gāai	*didn't go out*
...同...	...tùhng ... (short for tùhng-màaih)	*...and ...*
好遲/夜/晏/至...	hóu chìh/yeh/ngaan ji ...	*till very late ...*
不過...	bāt-gwo ...	*but ...*

 Conversation 1

Frank and Shuk-ling meet on Monday. They talk about what they did at the weekend.

1 Who likes doing exercises, and who doesn't like football?

Frank	Shuhk-lìhng, néih jāu-muht jouh-mē aa?
Shuk-ling	Sīng-kèih-luhk ngóh hóu-chíh-ji héi-sān, móuh-chēut-gāai, hái ūk-kéi duhk-Yīng-mán. Chàhm-yāt ngóh-tùhng aa-Marc heui-tái-hei.
Frank	Hóu-m̀h-hóu-tái aa?
Shuk-ling	Hóu aa. Gám néih Sīng-kèih-luhk-yāt jouh-mē aa?
Frank	Ngóh Sīng-kèih-luhk jīu-tàuh-jóu fāan-gūng. Hah-jau tùhng Issac dá yúh-móuh-káuh. Sīng-keìh-yaht heui cháai-dāan-chē.
Shuk-ling	Néih jūng-m̀h-jūng-yi dá bīng-pōng-bō gaa?
Frank	Jūng-yi. Néih-nē?
Shuk-ling	Jūng-yi. Bāt-gwo ngóh m̀h-jūng-yi tek-jyū-kàuh.

2 Look for the Cantonese equivalents for the following sentences. Note the tense.
- **a** I got up late.
- **b** I went to the cinema.
- **c** And you? What did you do at the weekend?
- **d** I worked in the morning.
- **e** I studied English at home.
- **f** I played table tennis.

3 Read the conversation and answer these questions.
- **a** What did Shuk-ling do on Saturday?
- **b** What about Frank?
- **c** What did Frank do on Sunday?
- **d** Does Shuk-ling like football?

4 09.03 Now listen to the lines from Conversation 1 and repeat. Then listen to Frank's lines and answer as if you were Shuk-ling.

Language discovery 1

1 Using the conversation to help you, decide how to say the following in Cantonese.
  a I didn't go out.
  b I studied English.
  c We watched a film.

2 What do the 'verb forms' *didn't*, *studied* and *watched* tell us about time?

THE PAST

In English, the above sentences are in the past tense, describing events that have already happened. In Unit 4, we covered topics relating to tense, and saw that Cantonese verbs have only one form. They do not change according to tense or number. Regardless of subject, tense and anything else, the verb will always remain unchanged, with no irregular forms. Cantonese indicates past events with tense markers, and words like *yesterday* show that an event took place in the past. There are several of these words in Conversation 1. What are they? Underline any that you can see in Conversation 1.

Here are some examples taken from Unit 4:

kàhm-yaht	*yesterday*	**chìhn-yaht**	*the day before yesterday*
seuhng-chi	*last time*	**ngāam-ngāam**	*just*
tàuh-sìn	*just now*	**yí-chìhn**	*before*

Seuhng (*last*) is a convenient word for indicating the past, as in **seuhng-chi**. Other examples include:

seuhng sīng-kèih	*last week*
seuhng sīng-kèih-yāt (yih, sāam ...)	*last Monday (Tuesday, Wednesday ...)*
seuhng go-yueht	*last month*

Interestingly, *last year* is **gauh-nín**; *the year before last* is **chìhn-nín**; *originally* is **bún-lòih**, and *then* is **gó-jahn-sih**.

3 Translate the following into Cantonese:
  a What did you do last Sunday?
  b I went to a concert last week.

4 In Conversation 1, find the Cantonese for the following:
  a Like.
  b Do you like table-tennis?
  c I don't like football.

Now you should know how to say *I like* (**jūng-yi** in Cantonese). If you don't like anything, you can precede the expression with **m̀h-**, making it **m̀h-jūng-yi**. To ask whether a person likes to listen to music or not, you can say: **Néih jūng-m̀h-jūng-yi tēng-yām-ngohk nē?**

If you want to mention somebody's name, just precede the above expressions with the name in question. So *Janette likes listening to music* will become **Janette jūng-yi tēng yām-ngohk**. If she doesn't, then the Cantonese will be **Janette m̀h-jūng-yi tēng-yām-ngohk**. To ask Janette whether she likes to listen to music or not, we will however need to include **néih**, the Cantonese will therefore become **Janette néih jūng-m̀h-jūng-yi tēng-yām-ngohk?**

Practice 1

1 **What did aa-Ming do last Monday? Use the correct verb to fill in the gaps.**

tái	pòuh	heui	hàahng

a Ngóh Sīng-keih-luhk heui yeh-_____.
b Ella-tùhng-ngóh chàahm-yaht heui _____-hei.
c Kéuih-deih seuhng-go-yueht _____-léui-hàhng.
d Ngóh jūng-yi _____-gūng-sī.

2 **Here are some of the things Yuk-yu wrote in her diary. Can you say what she did?**

a Tùhng Joshua hàahng-gūng-sī.
b Ngóh heoi dá yúh-móuh-káuh.
c Cháai-dāan-chē tùhng yeh-pòuh.
d Tùhng Grace heui-tái-hei.
e Ngóh kàhm-yaht dá-làahm-kàuh.
f Ngóh jūng-yi yeh-pòuh

3 **Matthew was asked to rate the activities listed in a survey.**
1 = **m̀h-jūng-yi**
2 = **jūng-yi**
3 = **hóu jūng-yi**

Read out what he writes down by starting the sentence with
Ngo . . . The first one has been done for you.

a dāan-chē (3) Ngóh hóu jūng-yi cháai-dāan-chē.
b jūk-kàuh (1)
c làahm-kàuh (2)
d waaht-syut (1)
e yeh-pòuh (3)
f tái-hei (2)

4 **Your friend Katie wants to know what you did yesterday.**

Katie	Néih kàhm-maáhn jouh māt-yéh?
You	*I went clubbing with a friend.*
Katie	Néih jūng-m̀h-jūng-yi dá-bīng-pōng-bō gaa?
You	*I like it very much.*

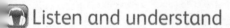 Listen and understand

1 09.04 **What did Anna do last week? Listen and choose the correct answer.**

a Ngóh chàhm-maáhn heui hàang-gūng-sī / yeh-pòuh.
b Sīng-kèih-yih tùhng pàhng-yáuh dá-làahm-kàuh / tek-jūk-kàuh.
c Sīng-kèih-sāam hái ūk-kéi cháai-dāan-chē / waaht-syut.
d Sīng-kèih-sei tùhng jèh-jē tái-hei / dá-yúh-móuh-kàuh.
e Sīng-kèih-lukh yeh-pòuh / heui-léui-hàhng.
f Sīng-kèih-yaht dá-làahm-kàuh / dá-yúh-móuh-kàuh.

2 09.05 **Listen to Christopher talking about his likes and dislikes. Try to score his opinions using the following key:**
1 = m̀h-jūng-yi
2 = jūng-yi
3 = hóu jūng-yi

a hàang-gūng-sī
b tái-hei
c dá-láam-kàuh
d yeh-pòuh
e cháai-dāan-chē
f tùhng pàhng-yáuh dá-yúh-móuh-káuh

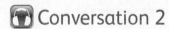
09.06 Megan and aa-Wing talk about their birthdays and when and where they were born.

1 Where were Megan and aa-Wing born?

Megan	Aa-Wing, néih géi-sìh sāang-yāt gaa?
aa-Wing	Yih-yuht yih-sahp-sei-houh.
Megan	Gám néih bīn-nìhn chēut-sai gaa?
aa-Wing	Yāt-gáu bāat-ngh-nìhn.
Megan	Ngóh-haih yāt-gáu bāat-bāat-nìhn bāat-yuht sāp-ngh-houh chēut-sai ge. Ngóh sīn-sāang hái yāt-gáu-gáu-gau-nìhn gáu-yuht gáu-hou chēut-sai.
aa-Wing	Néih-hái bīn-douh chēut-sai gaa?
Megan	Ngóh-haih Yīng-gwok chēut-sai ge, néih-nē?
aa-Wing	Ngóh-hái Méih-gwok chēut-sai gaa.
Megan	Néih haih-m̀h-haih hái gó-douh duhk-syū gaa?
aa-Wing	Haih-aa. Hái gó-douh yuh-dóu ngóh tai-tái Christina ge.
Megan	Gám néih-deih géi-sìh git-fān gaa?
aa-Wing	Ngóh-deih gauh-nìhn git-fān ge

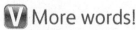 More words!

géi-sìh	*when*	**sāang-yāht**	*birthday*
bīn-nìhn	*which year*	**chēut-sai**	*be born*
gó-douh	*there*	**duhk-syū**	*study*
yuh-dóu	*meet*	**tai-tái**	*wife* (see unit 2)
gauh-nín	*last year*	**git-fān**	*get married*

2 Match the Cantonese and the English.

a Néih géi-sìh sāang-yaht gaa?   **1** Where were you born?
b Néih géi-sìh chēut-sai ge-nē?   **2** When did you get married?
c Néih-hái bīn-douh chēut-sai gaa?   **3** When is your birthday?
d Néih géi-sìh git-fān gaa?   **4** Did you study there?
e Néi haih-m̀h-haih hái gó-douh dūk-syū gaa?   **5** When were you born?

3 Read and listen to the conversation again, and answer True (T) or False (F).

a Aa-Wing's birthday is on 24th February.
b Megan was born on 15th August 1988.
c Aa-Wing met Christina on a holiday.
d He got married this year.

Language discovery 2

1 In the conversation, find the phrases that mean:

    a I was born   **c** I met my wife

    b My husband was born   **d** I got married

What did you notice? How is the past action expressed in Cantonese? Give at least three phrases that indicate a past event.

By now, you should know that Cantonese needs to use a 'past marker' to indicate past events. Verbs do not have such a function. Here are some examples:

Ngóh chēut-sai	literally *I born*
Ngóh haih *yāt-gáu baat-baat-nìhn* chēut-sai.	*I was born in 1988.*
Ngóh sīn-sāang chēut-sai	literally *My husband born*
Ngóh sīn-sāang haih *yāt-gáu chāt-gáu-nìhn* chēut-sai.	*My husband was born in 1979.*
Ngóh duhk-syū	literally *I study*
Ngóh duhk-*yùhn* syū.	*I finished my studies.*
Ngóh git-fān	literally *I marry*
Ngóh *gauh-nìhn* git-fān.	*I got married last year.*

2 Compare the following two sets of dialogues. Which set has shorter answers?

Set 1

Q	**Néih géi-sìh sāang-yāt gaa?**	*When is your birthday?*
A	**Yih-yuht yih-sahp-sei-houh.**	*24th February.*
Q	**Néih-deih géi-sìh git-fān gaa?**	*When did you get married?*
A	**Gauh-nìhn aa.**	*Last year.*

Set 2

Q	**Néih géi-sìh sāang-yaht gaa?**	*When was your birthday?*
A	**Ngóh yih-yueht yih-sahp-sei-houh sāang-yāt gaa.**	*I was born on 24th February.*
Q	**Néih-deih géi-sìh git-fān gaa?**	*When did you get married?*
A	**Ngóh-deih haih gauh-nình gīt-fān ge.**	*We got married last year.*

Bingo! The answers in Set 1 are shorter than those in Set 2. As in English, when we casually respond to queries, we do not necessarily need to repeat any word from a question. By and large, a short and succinct answer is not simply acceptable but can be rather welcome.

If you are wondering how to shorten an answer, study the two examples in Set 1. The basic rule is to give only the information you are asked for without repeating any words from the questions – as you do in English.

 Practice 2

1 Re-arrange the sentences to form a dialogue. Start with 1.

___ Yāt-gáu baat-sāam-nìhn.
_1_ Néih géi-sìh sāang-yāt nē?
___ Sahp-yāt yuht sahp-ńgh-houh.
___ Hái-bīn-douh nē?
___ Bīn-nìhn chēut-sai nē?
___ Hái-Yīng-gwok.

2 Complete the sentences with the correct verb from the box.

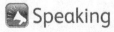

| git-fān | yuh-dóu | duhk | chēut-sai |

a Ngóh haih luhk-yueht chāt-houh hái Yīng-gwok _____.
b Néih haih yāt-gáu-gáu-sei-nìhn hái daaih-hohk _____-syū.
c William haih hái daaih-hohk _____ Kate.
d Kéuih-deih yāt-gáu-gáu-sāam-nìhn _____.

daaih-hohk *university*

Speaking

Answer these questions about yourself.

a Néih géi-sìh sāang-yāt aa?
b Néih géi-sìh cēut-sai gaa?
c Néih hái bīn-douh cēut-sai nē?
d Néih bīn-nìhn hái daaih-hohk duhk-syū nē?
e Néih géi-sìh bāt-yihp nē?
f Néih hái-bīn-douh fāan-gūng nē?

> **DON'T FORGET**
> **Bīn-douh?** *Where?*;
> **Bīn-nìhn?** *Which year?*;
> **bāt-yihp** *graduated*

Reading

1 Luca wants to visit China. He needs a visa and has obtained one from the China Travel Service (Hong Kong) Limited. The form he has is all in Chinese characters. He determines to learn to read the first four items.

a 姓名 name
b 性別 gender
c 出生日期 date of birth
d 出生地點／出生地点 place of birth

2 Fill out the form with your details (in either English or Chinese).

姓名 sing-mìhng	性別 sing-biht	出生日期 chēut-sāng yaht-kèih	出生地點 chēut-sāng deih-dím

Test yourself

1 Choose the right word to complete the sentences.

hàang	dá	tek	cháai

a Càahm-yāt ngóh heui _____-gūng-sī.
b Seuhng-go sīng-kèih-yāt, aa-Sam tùhng-ngòih _____-làahm-kàuh.
c Jāu-muht ngóh-deih _____-jūk-kàuh.
d Seuhng-go sīng-kèih ngóh tùhng kéuih-deih _____-dāan-chē.

2 09.07 In an interview with a journalist, Jacob, from New Zealand, talks about himself. Listen and note the information.

a Date and place of birth:
b Place of residence:
c Previous place of work:
d Current job:

SELF CHECK

I CAN ...
... talk about past events.
... say what I like or dislike.
... give biographical information.

10

今晚有咩節目？

Gām-máahn yáuh-mē jit-muhk?

What are your plans tonight?

In this unit you will learn how to:
▶ *talk about future plans.*
▶ *arrange to meet someone.*
▶ *make invitations.*
▶ *accept and decline an invitation.*

CEFR (A2): *Can discuss what to do, where to go and make arrangements to meet; can accept and decline invitations.*

 節日 Jit-yaht *Festivals*

Jit-yaht (*festivals*) and **hing-dín** (*celebrations*) reflect Hong Kong's unique fusion of Eastern and Western influences, adding to the richness and diversity of the city. The most significant Chinese festival may well be **lùhng-lihk sān-nìhn** (*the Chinese Lunar New Year*). Other well-known festivals include the Dragon Boat Festival, with its organized dragon boat races, and **Jūng-chāu-jit** (*Mid-Autumn Festival*) with its Lantern Carnivals. Of course, one cannot ignore the very local Hong Kong **Cheung-Chau Bun** Festival which has been ranked by Time.com, an American online magazine, as one of the world's 'Top 10 Quirky Local Festivals'.

Hong Kongers also honour Easter and **Sing-daan-jit** (*Christmas*), and have fun on **Chìhng-yàhn-jit** (*Valentine's Day*) and Halloween, making the land a truly vibrant Asian world city in China.

Nowadays, during the festivals, however, many people take the opportunity to have a holiday away from home or to visit family. People will therefore ask each other **Fuhk-wuht-jit néih wui-heui bīn (dou) aa?** (*Where are you going to go at Easter?*); **Néih-yáuh-mē jit-muhk aa?** (*What plans do you have?*); or **Néih jéun-beih heui-bīn aa?** (*Where are you planning to go?*).

 What is the Cantonese for *festival*?

Vocabulary builder

10.01 **Look at the following phrases, used in the conversation. Note their meanings and fill in the gaps to complete the phrases. Try pronouncing each word on your own. Then listen to the audio, and try to imitate the sounds as closely as you can.**

慶典 *HING-DÍN* CELEBRATIONS

邀請	yīu-chéng	*an invitation*
派對	paai-deui	*a party*
生日	sāang-yaht	*a birthday*
畢業	bāt-yihp	*graduation*
紀念日	géi-lihm-yāt	*an anniversary*
晚飯	máahn-faahn	*a dinner*
慶祝	hing-jūk	*to celebrate*

將來 *JĒUNG-LÒIH* IN THE FUTURE

今晚	gām-maahn	*tonight*
聽日	tīng-yaht	*tomorrow*
後日	hauh-yaht	*the day after tomorrow*
下星期一	hah sīng-kèih-yāt	*next Monday*
下星期	hah sīng-kèih	*_____ week*
下個月	hah go-yuht	*next month*
出年	chēut-nìhn	*_____ year*

生詞 *SĀANG-CHÌH* NEW EXPRESSIONS

…有咩節目/計劃?	… yáuh-mē jit-muhk/ gai-waahk?	*… any plans for entertainment?*
去佢(屋企)開 party.	Heui-kéuih (ūk-kéi) hōi party?	literally *Go to (his home) to have party.*
(大學)畢業。	(daaih-hohk) bāt-yihp	*(university) graduation*
冇計劃喎	móuh gai-waahk wo	*no plans*
點解你咁問呢?	Dím-gáai néih gám-maahn nē?	*Why do you ask?*
會…	wui …	*will …*
出去食飯	chēut-heui sihk-faahn	*eat out* (literally *go out to have dinner*)
…打算…	… dā-syun …	*… intend …*
去邊度(食飯)?	Heui bīn-douh (sihk-faahn)?	literally *… where to go (have dinner)?*
旋轉餐廳	syùhn-jyun-chāan-tēng	*The Revolving Restaurant*
…或者…	… waahk-jé …	*or, perhaps*
海鮮酒家	hói-sīn-jáu-gā	*the Seafood Restaurant*
…去過…?	… heui-gwo …?	*Have (you) been …?*

...邊間...	... bīn-gāan ...?	Which one ...?
...兩間都去過	... lèuhng-gāan dōu heui-gwo	... have been in both of them
...都...	... dōu ...	... also ... (literally have been)
自助餐	jih-jouh-chāan	buffet
...比較(平/多)	... béi-gaau (pèhng/dō)	... comparatively (cheaper/more)
啲	dī	a little bit
而且	yìh-ché	moreover
選擇	syún-jaahk	choices
咁就	gám jauh	if so (let us/me....)
一齊去...	yāt-chaìh-heui	go together ...
幾點?	Gēi-dím?	What time?
喺邊度等呢?	Hái bīn-douh dáng nē?	Where to meet?
喺門口等	hái mùhn-háu dáng	wait at the door
打電話	dā dihn-wā	telephone, call
訂檯	dehng-tói	reserve a table

 Conversation 1

10.02 Charlotte and two of her friends talk about their plans for tonight.

1 Listen and answer the questions. Who's going to a party tonight, and who has no plans?

Charlotte	Oliver, néih gām-máahn yáuh-mē jit-muhk aa?
Oliver	Ngóh heui Karen ūk-kéi hōi-party, hīng-jūk kéuih daaih-hohk bāt-yihp.
Charlotte	Néih-nē, Sophie, néih gām-máahn yáuh-mē gai-waahk?
Sophie	Móuh-mē gai-waahk wo.
Charlotte	Gām-yaht haih Benjamin ge sāang-yaht, ngóh-deih wui chēut-heui sihk-faahn hīng-jūk, néih làih-m̀h-làih aa?
Sophie	Hóu-aa. Néih-deih dá-syun heui bīn-douh sihk-fāan aa?
Charlotte	Syuhn-jyún-cāan-tēng, waahk-jé Hói-sīn-jáu-gā laa. Néih heui-gwo-bīn-gāan aa?
Sophie	Léuhng-gāan dōu heui-gwo. Syuhn-jyún chāan-tēng ge jih-jouh-chāan béi-gaau pèhng-dī, syún-jaahk béi-gaau dō dī.
Charlotte	Gám-jauh heui Syuhn-jyun chāan-tēng laa.
Sophie	Gēi-dím? Hái bīn-douh-dāng nē?
Charlotte	Chāt-dím-bun hái chāan-tēng mùhn-háu-dāng, hóu-m̀h-hóu aa?
Sophie	Hóu-aa.
Charlotte	Gám ngóh heui dá-dihn-wā dehng-tói laa.

> **LANGUAGE TIP**
> *Party* is a more commonly used word than its Chinese translation **paai-deui**.

Buffet is used as frequently as its Chinese counterpart **jih-jouh-chāan**.

Restaurant can be translated as **jáu-làuh** (literally *wine-building*), **jáu-gā** (literally *wine-home*), and **chāan-tēng** (which usually means *a Western restaurant*).

2 Match the questions and the answers.

a Néih gām-máahn yáuh-mē jit-muhk aa, Karen?

b Hái bīn-douh dáng nē?

c Néih deih dā-syun heui bīn aa?

d Néih heui-gwo-bīn-gāan aa?

1 Léuhng-gāan dōu heui-gwo.

2 Ngóh-deih wui-heui jáu-lau sihk faahn.

3 Ngóh heui Oliver ūk-kéi hōi-party.

4 Hái chāan-tēng múhn-háu dáng laa.

3 Read or listen to the conversation again and answer these questions.

a Why is today special to Benjamin?

b Which of the two restaurants is the better choice? Why?

c What time and where do Charlotte and Sophie arrange to meet?

Language discovery 1

1 Look back at Conversation 1. What is the Cantonese for these phrases?

a What are your plans for tonight?

b I'm going to phone.

FUTURE EVENTS

By now, you should have got used to the fact that Cantonese verbs only have one form. They will remain the same regardless of mood, subject, and tense. To indicate future events, we have to use time markers, some of which you learnt in Unit 4 and some in this unit. Can you give the English equivalents of the following?

tīng-yaht	_____	**hauh-yāht**	_____
hah-chi	*next time*	**gāam-máahn**	_____

Hah (*next*) is a convenient word for indicating the future, as in **hah-chi** (*next time*). Some more examples are:

hah Sīng-kèih	*next week*
hah Sīng-kèih-yāt (yih, sāam . . .)	*next Monday (Tuesday, Wednesday . . .)*
hah go-yuht	*next month*

Interestingly, *next year* is **chēut-nín**.

2 Read the paragraph on festivals and Conversation 1. Can you identify and underline expressions that indicate upcoming events? What are they?

They are **gai-waahk** (*a plan/to plan*), **dá-syun** (*to intend*; literally *calculate*), **jéun-beih** (*plan*; literally *ready*), **wúih** (*will/shall*), **séung** (*want, hope*), and **heui** (*to be*) as in these examples:

Néih yáuh-mē gai-waahk?	*What are your plans?*
Néih-deih dá-syùhn heui bīn-douh sihk-faahn aa?	*Where do you plan to have dinner?*
Néih jéun-beih heui-bīn aa?	*Where are you planning to go?*
Fuhk-wuht-jit néih wúih-heui bīn aa?	*Where will you go at Easter?*
Sing-daan-jit néih séung-heui bīn nē?	*Where would you like to go at Christmas?*
Gám ngóh heui dā dihn-wá dehng-toih laa.	*I am calling to reserve a table.*

LANGUAGE TIP

Heui has two meanings in this unit, *going to* and *to be*.

COMPARING THINGS

To mention only one item when comparing two things, we use **béi-gaau** (*compare*) and add **dī** (*a little*) to any adjective used, as in:

Jih-joh-chāan béi-gaau ping-dī.	*The buffet is comparatively cheaper.*
Jih-joh-chāan ge syún-jaahk béi-gaau dō-dī.	*There are more choices in buffets.*

To make a comparison between two things, we can use the verb **béi** (*compare*):

Jih-joh-chāan béi hói-sīn chāan pèhng.	*The buffet is cheaper than the seafood dinner.*
Hói-sīn béi dím-sām gwaai.	*Seafood is more expensive than dim sum.*

Note the comparative forms:

hóu	*good*	**hóu-dī**	*better*
pèhng	*cheap*	**pèhng-dī**	*cheaper*
gwai	*expensive*	**gwai-dī**	*more expensive*
daaih	*big*	**daaih-dī**	*bigger*
sai	*small*	**sai-dī**	*smaller*

Practice 1

1 **Read the following sentence pairs carefully. Put a tick against those that correctly use wui, jéun-beih, and dā-syun.**
   a Edward gām-yaht wui-heui Yīng-gwōk.
      Edward hóu-faai wúi-heui Yīng-gwōk.
   b Báh-bā jéun-beih chēut-huei-sihk-faahn.
      Báh-bā jéun-beih seuhng-Sīng-kèi-sāam chēut-huei-sihk-faahn.
   c Diane dā-syun hah-Sīng-kèih-yāt hing-jūk sāang-yāt.
      Diane dā-syun seuhng-Sīng-kèih-yāt hing-jūk sāang-yāt.

2 **Use the following words to make comparisons. Make use of the glossary if necessary.**
   a ge-fē – hóu – chàh
   b ngh-sīng jáu-dīm – gwaai – leuhng-sīng jáu-dim
   c faai-chāan-dim – pehng – hōi-sīn jáu-gā
   d gūng-gūng – daaih – bàh-bāa
   e sai-louh-jái – sai – pòh-pó

3 **Match each question with its logical answer.**
   a . . . dā-syuhn heui bīn-douh   1 . . . Móuh mē gai-waahk wo.
      sihk-faahn aa?   2 . . . heui-gwo.
   b . . . m̀h-séung heui Hōi-sīn jáu-gā?   3 . . . waak-jé Syùhn-jyun-
   c . . . yáuh-mē gai-waahk?   cāan-tēng laa.
   d . . . heui-gwo-meih aa?   4 . . . hóu-gwai gaa.

4 **Use what you know to answer these questions about yourself.**
   a Néih sān-nìhn jéun-beih jouh-mē nē?
   b Néih Sing-daan-jit wui jouh mē nē?
   c Néih dā-syun heui bīn-douh gwo-sāang-yāt nē?

V gwo-sāang-yāt *celebrate one's birthday* (literally *pass birthday*)

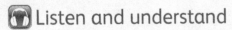

1 10.03 **Mei-yi is having a conversation with her friends Siu-ling and Hoi-lam. They talk about the plans they have for this evening. Listen and identify their planned activities. Put down M for Mei-yi, S for Siu-ling, and H for Hoi-lam. You may need to use more than one letter for some answers.**

　a heui-party　　　　　**d** Hói-sīn jáu-gā

　b sāang-yāt　　　　　**e** dá-dihn-wā

　c sihk-faahn

2 10.04 **Fan-fong asks Gim-hung what he and his partner are going to do at Easter. Listen and answer true (T) or false (F).**

　a Kim-hùhng and his partner are going to China at Easter.

　b They are going to be four days in Shanghai and three days in Beijing.

　c Fān-fōng knows Shanghai very well, but she doesn't know anything about Beijing.

　d She doesn't have money to go on holiday.

3 10.05 **Kim-hung and his wife Yun-yi are checking two hotels for their stay in Seuhng-hói. Listen and complete the missing words.**

Kim-hung	Nī léuhng-gān jáu-dim bīn-gān béi-gaau _____ nē?
Yun-yi	Seuhng-hói daaih-faahn-dim béi Sān-yuht jáu-dim _____-dī.
Kim-hung	Haih-aa, Seuhng-hói daaih-faahn-dim dī-yéh hóu-_____-dī.
Yun-yi	Seuhng-hói daaih-faahn-dim hóu _____, ngóh douh-haih jūng-yi _____-dī, _____-dī ge Sān-yueht jáu-dim.

114

🎧 Conversation 2

10.06 *Lu-lu phones Ga-ga and then Chi-ming to invite them to her graduation party.*

1 Listen and answer the question. Who accepts the invitation and who declines it?

Ga-ga	Wai. Wán-bīn-wái?
Lu-lu	Haa-lo, chéng-maahn Gā-gā haih-m̀h-haih-douh aa?
Ga-ga	Luh-luh, ngóh-haih Gā-gā aa. Néih-hóu maa?
Lu-lu	Ngóh hóu-hóu. Ngóh dā-dihn-wá làih haih-séung yīu-chéng néih hah Sīng-kèih-luhk heui-party gé. Hing-jūk ngóh daaih-hohk bāt-yihp.
Ga-ga	Hóu-aa! Hái-bīn-douh hōi aa?
Lu-lu	Haih ngóh daaih-hohk gó-douh aa. Jīu-tàuh-jóu sahp-yāt-dím.
Ga-ga	Hóu-aa, gám Sing-kèih-luhk gin-laa.
After a while . . .	
Chi-ming	Hā-lóu
Lu-lu	Wái, Chi-ming, ngóh haih Lū-lùh aa. Ngóh dā-dihn-wá laìh haih séung-chéng néih hah Sīng-kèih-luhk heui ngóh-gē bāt-yihp party gaa.
Chi-ming	Dō-jeh néih aa, Lū-lùh. Daahn-haih ngóh m̀h laìh-dāk aa. Yān-waih ngóh m̀h-haih hōu syū-fuhk, yáuh-dī gám-mouh. Jān-haih deui-m̀h-jyuh laa.
Lu-lu	M̀h-gán-yiu, gám hah-chi joi-chéng néih laa.

🔤 More words!

wái	*hello* (mostly used in telephone calls)
Wán-bīn-wái?	*Who are you looking for?*
dá-dihn-wá	*call* (literally *hit the telephone*)
séung-yīu-chéng	*would like to invite* (literally *want to invite*)
chéng	*invite* (short for *yīu-chéng*)
joi-chéng	*invite again* (literally *again invite*)
. . . hái-m̀h-hài-douh . . .?	*Is . . . there?* (literally *be-not-be there*)
dō-jeh	*thank you*

Hái bīn-douh hōi?	*Where is it to be held?* (literally *be where open?*)
Jīu-tàuh-jóu	*morning* (see Unit 9)
Sīng-kèih-luhk gin . . .	*See you on Saturday . . .* (literally *Saturday see . . . !*)
daahn-haih	*but*
m̀h laìh-dāk	*cannot come*
yān-waih	*because*
m̀h-haih hóu-syū-fuhk	*not quite well* (literally *no-yes very-comfortable*)
yáuh-dī gám-mouh	*have a bit of a cold*
jān-haih	*indeed*
m̀h-gán-yiu	*doesn't matter, never mind*

2 **Match the Cantonese with the English.**

a Haih bīn-douh hōi-nē?

b Ngóh yáuh-dī gám-mouh.

c Gā-gā hái-m̀h-hái-douh aa?

d Ngóh dā-dihn-wá-lai haih
   séung yiu-chéng néih . . .

e Ngóh m̀h-haih hóu syū-fuhk

1 I am calling to invite you . . .

2 I'm not well.

3 Where is it going to be held?

4 I have a cold.

5 Is Gaa-gaa there?

3 **Listen to the conversation again, then complete the
   information.**

a Lu-lu's party is next _____ (day).

b The party is in _____ (place), at _____ (time).

c Sa-sa can't come to the party because _____, and she _____.

💡 Language discovery 2

1 **Which phrase in the conversation means** *I'm calling to invite
   you . . .* **?**

DÁ

Dá has multiple meanings. When it pairs up with **dihn-wá** (*telephone*), it
means *call*. On some occasions, it simply means *hit* as in **kéuih-dā-ngóh**
(*he hits me*).

2 **Which phrase in the conversation means** *because I am not very
   well . . .* **?**

因為 *YĀN-WAIH*

Yān-waih (*because*) is a convenient word to express cause and effect, as in these examples:

Ngóh m̀h làih-dāk yān-waih ngóh m̀h syū-fūk.	*I can't come because I'm not well.*
Ngóh hóu tóu-ngoh yān-waih ngóh móuh sihk-faahn.	*I am hungry because I haven't eaten.* (literally *I am hungry because I haven't had dinner.*)
Ngóh tēng-m̀h-dóu néih-ge dihn-wá yān-waih ngóh m̀h-hái ūk-kéi.	*I didn't take your call because I was not at home.* (literally *I did not hear your telephone because I am not at home.*)

 Practice 2

1 Re-arrange the sentences to form a dialogue. Start with 1.

___ Ngóh haih Daaih-wàh, dā-dihn-wá laìh haih-séung yiu-chéng-néih laìh-ngóh douh hōi party.

___ M̀g-gán-yiu, hah-chi joi-chéng néih laa.

_1_ Hā-lóu, haih-m̀h-háih Gā-fāi aa?

___ Deui-m̀h-jyuh, ngóh m̀h-làih-dāk aa. Ngóh hóu-mòhng aa.

___ Ngóh haih Gā-fāi aa. Wán-bīn-wái?

 haih-nh-haih *is it?*; mòhng *busy*

2 Use Ngóh-m̀h-heui (*I can't go*) and yān-waih (*because*) to make logical sentences out of the following fragments.

a sìhk jih-jouh-chāan – hóu-gwai

b Hōi-sīn jáu-gā sihk-faahn – m̀h-hóu-sihk

c néih ūk-kéi – hóu-mòhng

d party – gám-mouh

3 Complete the sentences with the appropriate word.

bāt-yihp   syū-fuhk   hing-jūk   bīn-douh   dā-dihn-wá

a Ngóh _____ laih haih-séung chéng-néih heui-party.

b _____ ngóh daaih-hohk _____.

c Haih _____ hōi aa?

d Deui-m̀h-jyuh, ngóh m̀h-_____ aa.

 4 10.07 Laap-wai phones Yuet-wah to invite her out. Where does he invite her and why can't she accept the invitation?

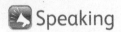 Speaking

A Cantonese-speaking **pàhng-yáuh** (*friend*) phones to invite you to
a dinner. Use what you know to take part in the conversation.

Pàhng-yáuh	Néih gām-maahn yáuh-mē jit-muhk?
You	*No, I don't have any plans.*
Pàhng-yáuh	Ngóh tùhng Waih-lìhng chēut-heui sihk-faahn, néih làih-ṁh-làih aa?
You	*Good. Which restaurants are you going to?*
Pàhng-yáuh	Heui Syùhn-jyún chāan-tēng, waahk-jé Hói-sīn jáu-gā. Néih heui-gwo-bīn-gāan aa?
You	*I have been in both. Hói-sīn jáu-gā is more expensive but the food is better.*
Pàhng-yáuh	Gám-jauh heui Hói-sīn jáu-gā laa. Chāt-dim-bun, hóu-ṁh-hóu aa?
You	*Good. Shall we meet at the entrance to the restaurant?*

 Reading

Read the birthday invitation card your Cantonese friend Suk-ping sent
you. Fill out the date, time, and venue.

> ### 邀請/邀请
> Yīu-chéng   Invitation
>
> ### 生日派對/生日派对
> Sāang-yaht paai-deui   Birthday Party
>
> **日期：八月八號（星期三）/八月八号（星期三）**
> Yaht-kèih: bāat-yuht bāat-houh (Sīng-kèih sāam)
> Date:
>
> **時間/时间：下午 三時正**
> Sìh-gaan: hah-ńgh sāam-sìh-jing
> Time:
>
> **地點/地点：我屋企**
> Deih-dím: Ngóh ūk-kéi
> Venue:

1 **When would you use each of the following words and phrases? Match the Cantonese and the English.**

a Géi-hóu aa.   **1** to express a reason
b Néih heui-bīn aa?   **2** to ask what someone's plan is
c Yān-waih.   **3** to express agreement
d Néih yáuh-mē jit-muhk? **4** to ask where someone is going

2 **Choose the right word for the following sentences.**

dá-syun	wui	gai-waahk	séung

a Néih gām-máahn yáuh-mē _____?
b Ngóh _____ heui-Méih-gwok.
c Ngóh _____ yīu-chéng néih.
d Néih-deih _____ heui-bīn-douh sīk-faahn aa?

3 10.08 **Where is Ka-wing being invited? Why can't he accept? Listen and find out.**

SELF CHECK

	I CAN . . .
○	. . . talk about future plans.
○	. . . arrange to meet someone.
○	. . . make invitations.
○	. . . accept and decline an invitation.

1 **Complete the dialogue with words from the list.**
    fó-géi   chàh-lòuh   séui-sīn   heui-yám-chàh
    a _____, m̀h-gōi màaih dāan.
    b Ngóh deih _____, sihk dím-sām.
    c Bīn-gān _____ yáuh jeui-hóu ge dím-sām nē?
    d Ngóh-séung yiu-wùh _____.

    Points: _____ /4

2 R3.01 **What are Jasmine and Ruth having? Listen to their conversation with the fo-gei (waiter) and note six food and drinks they mention.**
    a hā-_____   d _____
    b _____   e _____
    c _____   f _____

    Points: _____ /6

3 **Translate the following sentences into Cantonese, using the expressions béi . . . ngóh, Séung . . . mē-nē?, and Juhng-séung . . .**
    a Please let me have the menu.
    b What would you like to eat?
    c In addition, I would like to have a glass of red wine.
    d Please let me have a plate of spring rolls.
    e What would you like to drink?
    f In addition, I would like to have some fried rice.

    Points: _____ /6

4 **Fill in the appropriate classifiers.**
    a Kéuih yiu _____ baahk-jáu.
    b M̀h-gōi-béi _____ baahk-choi ngóh laa.
    c Yāt-_____ hei-séui, m̀h-gōi.
    d M̀h-gōi léuhng _____ hùhng-dáu-sā.
    e M̀h-gōi-béi _____ hēung-pín
    f Juhng-yiu yāt-_____ hā-gáau tim.

    Points: _____ /6

5 **What questions would you ask to get these replies? Use Géi-dim, Dím-yéung, or Hái bīn-douh to start your questions.**
   a Ngóh gáu-dím fāan-gūng.
   b Ngóh daap bā-sí fāan-gūng.
   c Ngóh tūng-sèuhng yeh-máahn baat-dím heui gihn-sān-sát.
   d Ngóh luhk-dím fong-gūng.

   Points: _____ /4

6 **Give the Cantonese equivalents of the following expressions.**
   a always
   b normally
   c usually
   d sometimes
   e never

   Points: _____ /5

7 R3.02 **Listen to Ga-wing asking Mei-gwan what she and her husband do at weekends. Decide if the following statements are true (T) or false (F).**
   a Mei-gwan and Jeun-yin get up very early on Saturdays.
   b After breakfast, Jeun-yin usually does exercises.
   c While Jeun-yin does exercises, Mei-gwan usually listens to music.
   d On Saturday afternoons, Mei-gwan sometimes watches television and sometimes plays tennis.
   e They usually go hiking on Sundays.

   Points: _____ /5

8 R3.03 **Listen to Christopher talking about his likes and dislikes. Try to score his opinions using the following key:**
   jeui jūng-yi = *like most*
   jūng-yi = *like*
   màh-má-déi = *so-so*
   m̀h-jūng-yi = *dislike*
   a tái dihn-sih
   b tēng yām-ngohk
   c yeh-pòuh
   d tek jūk-kàuh
   e jouh wahn-duhng
   f tùhng pàhng-yáuh hàahng-gāai

   Points: _____ /6

9 Translate the following sentences into Cantonese.
   a I went to the cinema.
   b I had an early breakfast.
   c I worked in the morning.
   d I played tennis.
   e What did you do last weekend?
   f I got up late.

Points: _____ /6

10 Give the Cantonese equivalents to the following past-tense markers.
   a yesterday   **d** the day before yesterday
   b last time   **e** last week
   c last year   **f** just now

Points: _____ /6

11 Match the Cantonese with the English.
   a Néih géi-sìh chēut-sai ge-nē?   **1** Where were you born?
   b Néih géi-sìh git-fān gaa?   **2** Did you study in the United
   c Néih haih-nh-haih hái   States?
       Méih-gwok duhk-syū gaa?   **3** When did you get married?
   d Néih-hái bīn-douh chēut-sai gaa?   **4** When is your birthday?
   e Néih gēi-sìh sāang-yaht gaa?   **5** When were you born?

Points: _____ /5

12 What questions would you ask to get these replies?
   a Ngóh sāam-yuht sāam-sahp yāt-houh sāang-yaht.
   b Ngóh hái yāt-gáu gáu-gáu nình chēut-sai.
   c Ngóh hái daaih-hohk jouh-yéh.
   d Ngóh hái yih-lìhng lìhng-baat nìhn git-fān.
   e Ngóh hái héung-góng chēut-sai.

Points: _____ /5

13 R3.04 **Listen to the conversation between Lai-ling and Suk-ting.
   Then match the questions with the answers.**
   a Néih gām-máahn yáuh-mē   **1** Hái chāan-tēng muhn-háu-
       jit-muhk ne?   dáng laa.
   b Hái bīn-douh dáng nē?   **2** Heui-gwo.
   c Néih deih dā-syun heui-bīn aa? **3** Móuh mē jit-muhk wo.
   d Néih heui-gwo maih gaa?   **4** Ngóh-deih-wui chēut-heui
                                             sihk-faan.

Points: _____ /4

14 Give the English equivalents of the following future time markers.

a ha go-yuet
b tīng-yaht
c cheut-nín
d haau-yat
e gaam-maan
f hah Sīng-kei yi

15 Complete the sentences with the appropriate expressions from the following list.

gai-waahk dā-syun jéun-beih wui séung heui

a Gám ngóh _____ dā-dihn-wá dehng-tói laa.
b Ngóh yìh-gā _____ chēut-mùhn háu.
c Jūng-chāu-jit néih _____-heui bīn aa?
d Néih _____-heui bīn-douh gwo Sing-daan aa?
e Néih _____ heui bīn-douh sihk-faahn aa?
f Néih gām-máahn yáuh-mē _____ aa?

16 Translate the following sentences using the expressions bei, bei-gaau, and yan-wai.

a Seafood is comparatively more expensive.
b Dim sum is cheaper than seafood.
c I can't come because I have a cold.
d There are more choices in buffets.
e Orange juice is tastier than apple juice.
f I don't want to eat because I'm not hungry.

Answer key

UNIT 1

Cantonese: Language discovery

1 Gwóng-dūng-yàhn; **2** country

Vocabulary builder

Hi/hello (there!); (How are) you?

Conversation 1

1 Chan (Cháhn), Lee (Léih)
2 a I **b** you **c** good morning **d** Miss **e** Mr
3 a How are you? **b** jóu-sáhn **c** I am very well **d** Not bad/Quite good
e géi-hóu, hóu-hóu

Language discovery 1

1 Néih **2** Ngóh

Practice 1

1 a néih **b** kéuih **c** ngóh-deih **d** kéuih **e** kéuih **f** kéuih-deih
2 Ngóh sing-Wòhng
3 a Néih-hóu!/Jóu-sàhn! **b** Ngóh-sing Chàhn. **c** Ngóh hóu-hóu!

Listen and understand

a Léih-táai/Léih-taai-táai **b** Chàhn-sīn-sāang **c** néuih-sih **d** síu-jé

Practice 2

a 4 Ms Chiu **b** 3 Mr Wong **c** 1 Miss Chan **d** 2 Mrs Chau **e** 5 Mrs Lau
What about forenames **2b b** (aa-)hòuh **c** (aa-)lìhng **d** aa-wáih **e** aa-fān
f aa-giht

Conversation 2

1 aa-Wáih, a woman
2 a introduce **b** This is **c** call **d** Call me **e** name **f** I am **g** How **h** very good

Language discovery 2

b nē **c** lāa **d** nē **e** āa

Practice 3

a nē **b** lāa **c** nē **d** aa **e** āa

Test yourself

1 a 3 **b** 5 **c** 1 **d** 6 **e** 7 **f** 4 **g** 2

2 a néih-nē **b** chīng-fū-aa **c** néih-ne **d** gwai-sing **e** Ngóh-haih **f** mē-méng-nē

3 a Chíng-máhn gwai-sing? **b** Ngóh hóu-hóu. **c** Ngóh láih-gaai-siuh.
d Chàhng-síu-jé, néih-hóu-maa? or Néih-hóu-maa, Chàhng-siu-jé.

UNIT 2

Hong Kongers: Language discovery

Néih yáuh-móuh

Vocabulary builder

a 3 **b** 4 **c** 1 **d** 5 **e** 2

Conversation 1

1 wuh-sih (nurse)

2 a Nèih yáuh-móuh jóuh-yéh aa? **b** Néih sīn-sāang jouh-mē aa? **c** Kéuih haih-go gīng-léih. **d** Kéuih-hái jūng-hohk gaau-syū.

3 a She teaches in a secondary school. **b** history **c** 20 **d** engineering

Language discovery 1

a haih **b** go **c** Ngóh yih-sahp-seui.

Learn more: Questions

c (a question)

Practice 1

a haih **b** x **c** haih, x **d** m̀h-haih

2 a Keuih nàahm-pàhng-yáuh haih-^ yih-sāang. **b** Ngóh gùhng-gūng haih- ^ lóuh-sī. **c** Keuih-^- jái yī-sahp-seui. **d** Ngóh haih-^ wuh-sih, haih yī-yún fāan-gūng.

3 a Ngóh-giu (your name). **b** Ngóh(your age) seui. **c** Ngóh-haih-go (your occupation). **d** Hái (your office venue) fāan-gūng.

Listen and understand

1 a 3, **b** 1, **c** 4, **d** 6, **e** 2, **f** 5

2 yi-sahp (seui); yi-sahp-yi (seui)

3 & 4 13 sahp(-sām); 14 sahp(-sei); 15 sahp(-ńgh); 17 (sahp-)chāt; 18 (sahp-)baat; 19 (sahp-)gáu; 22 (yih-sahp-)yih

5 a 1, 11 (yāt, sahp-yāt) **b** 2, 12 (yih, sahp-yih) **c** 3, 13 (sāam, sahp-sāam) **d** 4, 14 (sei, sahp-sei) **e** 5, 15 (ńgh, sāp-ńgh) **f** 6, 16 (luhk, sahp-luhk) **g** 7, 17 (chāt, sahp-chāt) **h** 8, 18 (baat, sahp-baat) **i** 9, 19 (gáu, sahp-gáu) **j** 1 0, 20 (sahp, yih-sahp)

Conversation 2

1 2 (one boy, one girl); four & two (respectively for the boy & girl)
2 a one (older) brother, one (younger) sister **b** tall and handsome;
c slim/thin

Language discovery 2

Ngóh-yáuh léuhng-go sai-louh.; Ngóh-yáuh yāt-go gòh-gō, yāt-go mùih-múi.

Practice 2

1 b yáuh-móuh, ngóh-yáuh, Móuh **c** Yáuh, ngóh-móuh **d** Yáuh, ngóh-yáuh.
Móuh, ngóh-móuh

Reading

one, two, three

Test yourself

1 a yáuh-móuh **b** haih **c** go, haih **d** mē-nē/māt-ye **e** mē, māt-ye
f haih-m̀h-haih
2 a 28 (yih-sahp-baat [seui]) **b** son-18 (Kéuih-gō-jái baat-seui.);
daughter-21(Kéuih-go-néui yih-sahp-yat-seui)

UNIT 3

Retail therapy: Language discovery

chín; Hong Kong dollars (góng-jí); Riminbi (yàhn-màhn-baih)

Vocabulary builder

clothing women; men

Conversation 1

1 shirt ((sēut)sāam)
2 a white (baahk-sīk), red (hùhng-sīk) **b** no **c** long (black) trousers
(hāk-sīk-ge chèuhng-fu)
3 a 3; **b** 5; **c** 4; **d** 1; **e** 2

Language discovery

1 may (I)?; Does it fit? (literally fit-not-fit?); m̀h

Practice

1 a Kéuih géi-daaih? **b** Néih géi-gōu? (for both tall and short) **c** Kéuih
géi-sai? **d** Néih géi-fèi? (for both fat and thin)
2 a nine blouses for women **b** three pairs of trousers **c** a pair of glasses
3 a May I try this grey shirt? **b** May I try that yellow sweater? **c** May I try
this pair of red trousers? **d** May I try that orange skirt/dress?

Speaking

1 a Gó-gihn sēut-sāam géi-dō-chín aa? **b** Néih yáuh-móuh luhk-sīk aa? **c** Néih yáuh-móuh sāam-sahp-yih máh aa? **d** Ngóh hó-m̀h-hó-yíh si-háh gó-tìuh kwàhn aa?

Listen and understand

1 (Numbers 31 to 99) 31 yāt; 32 sahp-yih 43 sāam 44 sei-sahp; 55 ngh-saph; 56 luhk; 67 luhk-sahp; 68 luhk-sahp; 69 gáu; 71 chāt-sahp; 72 sahp-yih; 73 chāt-sahp-sāam; 84 sei; 85 baat-sahp-ngh; 86 baat-sahp-luhk; 97 gāu-sahp-chāt; 98 gāu-sahp-baat;
2 (Numbers 1–99) 1 yāt; 2 yih; 3 sāam; 4 sei; 5 ngh; 6 luhk; 7 chāt; 8 baat; 9 gáu; 10 sahp; 11 sahp-yāt; 12 sahp-yih; 13 sahp-sāam; 14 sahp-sei; 15 sahp-ngh; 16 sahp-luhk; 17 sahp-chāt; 18 sahp-baat; 19 sahp-gáu; 20 yih-sahp; 21 yih-sahp-yār; 22 yih-sahp-yih; and so on to **30**; 31 sāam-sahp-yāt; 32 sāam-sahp-yih; and so on to **40**; 41 sei-saph-yāt; and so on to **50**; 50 ngh-sahp; and so on to **60**; 60 luhk-sahp; 70 chāt-sahp; 80 bāat-sahp; 90 gáu-sahp; and so on to **99**; 99 gáu-sahp-gáu
3 (Numbers 100–999) 103 sāam 120 yāt-baak; 200 baak; 204 lìhng; 261 yih-baak; 300 baak; 345 sāam-baak 430 sāam-sahp; 562 luhk-sahp-yih; 670 luhk-baak 710 chāt-baak yāt-sahp; 890 baat-baak gāu-sahp
4 a yāt-baak-luhk-sahp-chāt (167) **b** ngh-baak-sāam-sahp-sei (534) **c** gāu-baak-chāt-sahp-yi (972) **d** sāam-baat-sahp-sāam (383) **e** yih-baak-sei-sahp-ngh (245) **f** yāt-cīn-sāam-baak (1,300)
5 a taai-daaih, sai-dī **b** taai-chèuhng, dyún-dī **c** taai-gwai, pèhng-dī **d** taai-dyún, chèuhng-dī

Speaking

1 Deui-m̀h-jyuh, gó-dī (hàih) géi-dō-chín aa?; Hóu-gwai aa, Néih hó-m̀h-hó-yíh gáam-ga aa?
2 Ngóh máaih-jó-kéuih laa.

Reading

1 chāt-jit 30 %; sei-jit 60 %; léuhng-jit 80 %
2 a dresses; **b** 10 %; **c** T-shirts

Test yourself

1 a Gó-dī-fu géi-dō-chín? Làahm-sihk gó-dī. **b** Ngóh-séung yiu sei-sahp-luhk maa. **c** Ngóh hó-m̀h-hó-yíh si-háh kéuih aa? **d** Sai-jóu-dī. **e** Nī-gihn sāam hóu ngāam-sān/ngóh.
2 Mary: yāt-gihn hùhng-sīk sēut-sāam, sāam-tìuh dyún-kwàhn, sei-deui-hàaih; John: yāt-deui ga-fēi-sik hàaih, léuhng-gihn ngoih-tou, yāt-gihn fūi-sīk lāang-sāam.

3 a yāt-baak-sei-sahp-yi **b** yih-baak-chāt-sahp-yāt **c** sāam-baak-baat-sahp-gáu **d** ńgh-baak-gáu-saph **e** chāt-baak luhk-sahp-chāt **f** yih-chīn-ńgh-baak; **g** sahp-maahn

Review 1

1 Néih, Ngóh, Ngóh, Ngóh, néih, Ngóh, Néih-, Ngóh;
2 a Néih-hóu **b** jóu-sāhn, néih-hóu **c** Ngóh sing- **d** Ngóh hóu-hóu **e** Ngóh dōu-géi-hóu
3 a taai-táai **b** síu-jé **c** sīn-sāang **d** néuih-sih
4 a 17 **b** 25 **c** 48 **d** 61 **e** 73 **f** 14
5 a haih **b** go **c** Ngóh yih-sahp-seui.
6 a Ngóh m̀h-haih go wuh-sih. **b** Néih haih-m̀h-haih gō wuh-sih? **c** Kéuih m̀h-haih go gei-jé. **d** Kéuih haih-m̀h-haih go gei-jé? **e** Néih m̀h-haih Jūng-gwok-yàhn. **f** Néih haih-m̀h-haih Jūng-gwok-yàhn?
7 a gihn **b** tìuh **c** deui
8 a Nī-dī fu **b** Gó-go yàhn **c** Nī-tìuh kwàhn **d** Gó-deui ngáahn-geng
9 a Nī-gihn-sāam géi-dō chin nē? **b** Néih yáuh-móuh sāam-sahp-baat-máah aa? **c** Ngóh hó-m̀h-hó-yi si-hah kéuih? **d** Gó-gihn hóu-ngāam-sān. **e** Ngāam-saai néih aa. **f** Ngóh-séung yiu-gihn baahk-sīk ge.

UNIT 4

Getting by in Hong Kong and the Chinese mainland:
Language discovery

síu-lèuhn

Vocabulary builder

the time: twelve, seven, five, six
days of the week: Monday, Tuesday, Thursday, Saturday

Language discovery

一 1, 二 2, 三 3, 四 4, 五 5, 六 6; (星期)日/(Sīng-kèih) yaht

Conversation 1

Tuesday 15th (sahp-ńgh houh, Sīng-kéih yih), 7 a.m. (seuhng-jau chāt-dím bun);
2 a 2, **b** 4, **c** 6, **d** 5, **e** 3, **f** 1
3 a Tuesday the 15th (sahp-ńgh houh, Sīng-kéih yih) **b** morning (seuhng-jau) **c** 7 a.m. (seuhng-jau chāt-dím) **d** 3 p.m. (hah-jau sāam-dím) **e** $HK 190 (yāt-baak gáu-sahp mān Góng-jí)

Language discovery 1

1 géi-dím; chāt-dím bun; sahp-yih-dím sāam

Time

1 seuhng-jau, hah-jau
3 seuhng-jau chāt-dím bun, hah-jau sāam-dím

Bun – half an hour

In Conversation 1: 7.30 (chāt-dím-bun);
4 a 13.30 hah-jau jāt-dím-bun, **b** 2.30 p.m. hah-jau leuhng-dím-bun,
c 6.30 a.m. seuhng-jau luhk-dím-bun, **d** 7.30 p.m. hah-jau chát-dím-bun

Practice

1 b 2.00 léuhng-dím (jūng) NOT yih-dím (jūng); **c** 3.00 sāam-dím (jūng);
d 4.00 sei-dím (jūng); **e** 5.00 nģh-dím (jūng); **f** 6.00 luhk-dím (jūng);
g 7.00 chāt-dím (jūng); **h** 8.00 baat-dím (jūng); **j** 10.00 sahp-dím (jūng);
k 11.00 sahp-yāt-dím (jūng); **l** 12.00 sahp-yih-dím (jūng);
2 a seuhng-jau dihng-haih hah-jau (aa)? **b** Ngóh-yiu chāt-dím-bun
gó-bāan –aa. **c** Géi-dím dou Gwóng-jāu (nē)?
3 Friday 12:00 Sīng-kèih-nģh jūng-nģh sahp-yih-dím; Tuesday 9:15
Sīng-kèih-yih seuhng-jau gáu-dím-sāam/jāt-go-gwāt/sahp-nģh-fān;
Sunday 24:00 Sīng-kèih-yaht nģh-yeh/lìhng-sàhn sahp-yih-dím

Speaking

a Ngóh-séung yiu-jēung heui-seuhng-hói ge fēi. **b** (Chéng-mahn) jeui-jóu
gó-bāan bā-sí géi-dím-hōi? **c** (Chéng-mahn) géi-dím dou Seung-hói (nē)?
d Ngóh-séung yiu-jēung lòih-wùih fēi.

Conversation 2

1 Cambridge 2.30 p.m. (hah-jau léuhng-dím-bun); Hong Kong 8.30 p.m.
(yeh-máahn baat-dím-bun);
2 a Haih-néih àah? **b** ngóh yíh-gīng jéun-beih-hóu heui . . . **c** Géi-dím nē?
d Géi-síh-làih (aa)? **e** Géi-dím-dou?

Language discovery 2

1 a Hēung-góng yìh-gā géi-dím aa?; **b** Ngóh-wui daap lìhng-sàhn
sahp-yih-dím gó bāan-gēi
2 present: yìh-gā, **past:** jéun-beih, **future:** wui, (shall/will)

Practice 2

1 Géi-sìh-làih (aa)?; Daap géi-dím bāan-chē (nē)?; Géi-dím dou-Lùhn-
dēun (nē)?
2 a wui; **b** yíh-gīng; **c** yìh-gā

Reading

1 exit; entrance; toilet; **2 a** exit; **b** entrance; **c** toilet

Writing

入口; 出口

Test yourself

1 a Sīng-kèih-yih sahp-yāt-dím sāam-go-gwāt/sei-sahp-ńgh-fāan **b** Sīng-kèih-ńgh yāt yāt-go-gwāt/sahp-ńgh-fāan **c** Sīng-kèih-yaht luhk-dím yāt-go-gwāt/sahp-ńgh-fāan **d** Sīng-kèih-yāt léuhng-dím-bun/sāam-sahp-fāan **e** Sīng-kèih-luhk ńgh-dím lìhng-yāt-fāan **f** Sīng-kèih-sei baat-dím yih-sahp-chāt-fāan **g** Sīng-kèih-sāam gáu-dím lìhng-baat-fāan
2 a sēung-chìhng; **b** wui-daap, lèih-hōi
3 a Thursday the 17th (sahp-chāt-houh, Sīng-kéih-sei) **b** 2.30 p.m. and 6.15 p.m. (hah-jau léuhng-dím-bun, hah-jau luhk-dím sāam) **c** 9.00 p.m. (Yeh-máahn gáu-dím)

UNIT 5

Where to stay: Language discovery

hotels (ńgh-sīng-kāp jáu-dim); guest houses (bān-gún); apartments (gūng-yuh); and hostels (léuih-gún).

Vocabulary builder

Hotel room: (single) room; (no) bathroom; (not include) breakfast

Conversation 1

1 5
2 a 2 **b** 4 **c** 1 **d** 3
3 a dāan-yàhn-fóng **b** HKD250 **c** included

Language discovery 1

a Ngóh-séung . . . **b** tùhng-màaih; **c** júng-guhng
Your turn: Ngóh-séung yiu-gāan fóng.
Your turn: Júng-guhng luhk-baak-sāam-sahp-ńgh-mān méih-gām.
The months: February, March, April, May, June, July, August, September, October, November

Practice 1

a 2; **b** 3; **c** 1
2 a Yih-yuht jih-sahp-sei-houh **b** chāt-yuht chāt-houh **c** sahp-yih-yuht yi-sahp-ńgh-houh

Listen and understand

1 a 00-852-364-32; **b** 0755-936-78 **c** 20-7942-271, ext 228

Speaking

You can either give a straight answer, or precede your answer with the expression Ngóh-go- sing/méng/dihn-wá . . . haih. . . .

Conversation 2

1 yes; jáu-dim chyùhn-múhn literally means 'the hotel is full'.
2 a 2; **b** 3; **c** 1

Language discovery 2

a Ngóh dehng-jó gāan sēung-yàhn-fóng. **b** Gām-yaht juhng yáuh-móuh fóng-hūng aa?

Practice 2

1 a dehng-jó; **b** yáuh-móuh **c** chīm-méng; **d** muhn
2 a gāan; **b** tìuh; **c** gāan

Speaking

a Ngóh-séung yiu-gāan sēung-yahn-fóng, luhk-yuht sahp-ńgh-houh, yiu yāt-go sīng-kèih. **b** Gāan-fóng géi-chín aa?; **c** Bāau-m̀h-baau jóu-cāan aa?

Reading and writing

a 2 **b** 3 **c** 1

Test yourself

1 a Matthew Cheung **b** Hong Kong 00 852 366 42 **c** single room
d 8th September **e** four nights
2 a Séung-yiu-gāan dāan-yàhn fóng? **b** Ngóh-gāan-fóng júng-guhng géi-dō-chín aa? **c** Néih-dihn-wá géi-dō-houh nē? **d** Gām-yaht juhng yáuh-móuh fóng-hūng aa?

UNIT 6

Sightseeing: Language discovery

yúhn; fuh-gahn; (chíng-mahn) dím-heui . . .

Vocabulary builder

Directions: where; right
Around town: bus

Conversation 1

1 two places: the bank (ngáhn-hóhng) and the museum (bok-mat-gúhn)
2 a 5; **b** 6; **c** 1; **d** 3; **e** 2; **f** 4
3 a the bank (ngàhn-hòhng) **b** the museum (bok-mat gúhn) **c** five minutes from here (haih nī-douh hàahng-heui ńgh-fān-jūng jauh-dou)
d on foot (hàahng)

Language discovery 1

a Yáuh-móuh ngàhn-hòhng aa?; **b** Bok-maht-gún hái-bīn-douh nē?

Practice 1

1 a Daaih-koi gwo-ngh-gāan daaih-hah jauh-dou. **b** Daaih-koi luhk-go jūng-tàuh jauh-dou. **c** Daaih-koi baat-chīn-maih jau-dou.

2 b Dím-yéung-heui Sō-hòuh?; Sō-hòuh dím-yéung-heui?; Sō-hòuh hái-bīn douh? **c** Dím-yéung-heui léuih-haak sēun-maahn jūng-sām?; Léuih-haak sēun-maahn jūng-sām dím-yéung-heui?; Léuih-haak sēun-maahn jūng-sām hái-bīn douh? **d** Dím-yéung-heui Màhn-móuh-míu?; Màhn-móuh-míu dím-yéung-heui?; Màhn-móuh-míu hái-bīn douh?

3 a gāak-lèih, jauh-dou **b** Bok-maht-gún, deui-mihn, jauh-dou **c** Bā-sí-júng-jaahm, yauh

4 a 3; **b** 2; **c** 1

5 a heung, jyun **b** gāak-lèih **c** jyun **d** chìhn-mihn

Conversation 2

1 MTR (Mass Transit Railway)

2 a Nathan Road **b** It's three streets away from here

Language discovery 2

a Néih-jyuh hái bīn-douh aa? or Néih-ge deih-jí ne? **b** Páau-máh-déi, bāat-sahp-bāat houh, sāam lóu, B joh. **c** Ngóh-jyuh-hái Wàh-Mèih-Laih.

Practice 2

1 a Wāan-jái, sahp-yāt-houh, ngh-láu **b** Páau-máh-déi, chāt-houh, A sāt **c** Nèih-dēun-dou, sāam-sahp-yih houh, luhk-láu, baat-joh

2 5, 1, 4, 2, 3, 6

3 b Ngóh jyuh-hái sāam-lóu.; **c** Ngóh jyuh-hái sahp-suhk-lóu.; **d** Ngóh jyuh-hái yih-sahp-jāt-lóu.

4 a Ngáhn-hòhng jauh-hái yeuhk-fòhng gaak-lèih. **b** Gwo sāam-tìuh gāai jauh-douh laa. **c** Hái nī-tìuh gāai heung chìhn-jóu, daih sei-gān jauh-haih laa.

Reading

a 2; **c** 3; **d** 1

Speaking

a Néih-jyuh hái bīn-douh aa?/Néih-ge deih-jí ne? **b** Haih-m̀h-haih hóu-yúhn aa? **c** Néih hó-m̀h-hó-yí jou-góng yāt-ci néih-go deih-ji aa? **d** Dím-heui-nē?

Test yourself

1 a haih-bīn douh; **b** Fuh-guhn; **c** dím-heui; **d** hauh-mihn
2 a Gāai-síh hái-léih jó-bihn. **b** Bā-síh júng-jaahm hái-néih chìn-mihn.
c Yáuh aa. Hàang-gwo sāam-gāan jauh-dou. **d** Hóu-káhn aa, hái gāai-síh
gaak-lèih.
3 Chíng/Chéng-mahn Daaih-sām-bā pàaih-fōng hái-bīhn-dou?; Haih-m̀h-
haih hóu-yúhn aa?; Ngóh dím-yéung-huei aa?; M̀h-gōi-saai, fuh-gahn
yáuh-móuh ngàhn-hóhng aa?

Review 2

1 a sāam-dím-sahp-nǵh **b** sāam-dim sei-sahp-nǵh-fān/sāam-dim
sāam-go-gwāt **c** baat-dím-sei-sahp-nǵh/baat-dím sāam-go-gwāt
d léuhng-dím sahp-nǵh-fān/léuhng-dím yāt-go-gwāt
2 a bun-yé sāam-dím **b** hah-jau luhk-dím **c** seuhng-jau baat-dím
d hah-jau nǵh-dím **f** lìhng-sàhn léuhng-dím **g** yeh-máahn sahp-yāt-dím
h seuhng-jau sahp-dím
3 b seuhng-jau baat-dím sahp-nǵh fān/sāam-go-jih; hah-jau luhk-dim
yih-saph fān **c** hah-jau léuhng-dīm; hah-jau sai-dim **d** lìhng-sàn sahp-yih-
dím; seuhng-jau chāt-dim
4 c yāt-dím yih/leuhng(-go-jih) **d** sei-dím sei(-go-jih) **e** chāt-dím chāt(-go-
jih) **f** sahp-dím-sahp(-go-jih) **g** sāam-dím sāam-go-gwāt **h** sai-dím
yāt-go-jih **i** sāam-dím yāt-go-gwāt **j** nǵh-dim nǵh(-go-jih) **k** gáu-dím
sāam(-go-jih) **l** sahp-yāt-dím-sahp-yāt
5 Man-git máaih yāt-jēung; Man-git Yih-sahp-luhk-(houh),
(Sīng-kéih-) sāam; Sau-piu-yun Seung-jau, haa-jau; Man-git Jeui-jóu,
gēi-dihm; Sau-piu-yun chāt-dím-bun
6 Yuk-ling sahp-juht nǵh-houh; Jip-doi-yun sēung-yàhn-fóng; Yuk-ling
dāan-yàhn-fóng; Jip-doi-yun jyuh géi-dō máahn, Yuk-ling Luhk-máahn
7 a Ngóh dehng-jó gān sēung-yàhn-fóng. **b** Ngóh máaih-jó léuhng gihn
sēut-sāam. **c** Ngóh juhng-séung heui Bāk-gīng. **d** Néih yáuh-móuh
fó-chē-fēi? **e** Bāau-m̀h-bāau jóu-chāan nē? **f** Júng-guhng géi-dō chín nē?
8 a 3, **b** 4, **c** 2, **d** 1
9 a daaih-koi **b** Gwo **c** gwo **d** Daaih-koi

UNIT 7

Eating out in Hong Kong: Language discovery

Bāk-gīng-choi, Seuhng-hói-choi, Sei-cyūn-choi, and Gwóng-dūng-choi;
food/cuisine

Conversation 1

1 Wendy; a plate of fried rice

2 a 3; **b** 5; **c** 4; **d** 6; **e** 2; **f** 1

3 a prawn crackers, barbecue pork, fried noodles, red wine, tap water, and red-bean soup **b** yes **c** jī-máh syut-gōu

Language discovery 1

1 a M̀h-gōi béi-go chāan-páai ngóh. **b** Séung-yám-dī mē-nē?
c Ngóh juhng-séung-yiu-dī chīng-séui tīm.

4 Ngóh juhng-séung yiu-būi ga-fē

5 a Ngóh-deih séung-yiu léuhng-būi chīng-séui. **b** Keui-dei séung-yám jáu.

Practice 1

1 a M̀h-gōi nógh-deih séung-yiu dī chīng-séui. **b** M̀h-gōi màaih-dāan.
c Ngóh séung-yiu- dī cháau-mihn. **d** Ngóh séung-yiu-dī jī-màh syut-gōu.

2 a Chíng-mahn **b** M̀h-gōi **c** Deui-m̀h-jyuh **d** M̀h-gōi-néih hó-m̀h-hó-yi

3 a būi **b** dihp **c** jī **d** wún

4 M̀h-gōi béi-go chāan-páai ngóh.; Ngóih-deih séung-yiu léuhng-wún jaahp-choi-tōng.; (Ngó-deih séung-yiu) yāt-jī huhgn-jáu. Juhng-séung yiu-dī syuet-gōu.

Listen and understand

1 prawn crackers (hā-pín), curry chicken (ga-léih-gāi), Chinese cabbage (baahk-choi), red-bean soup (huhng-dáu-sā), ice cream (syut-gōu), soft drink (hei-séui)

2 chāan-jáu (table wine); hùhng-jáu (red wine); hei-séui (soft drink);
3 a F **b** I **c** F **d** I

Conversation 2

1 Josephine, Kam-leung (Aslan's brother)

2 a sā-lēut **b** cháang-jāp **c** ga-fē-gā-náaih **d** sāam-màhn-jih **e** jī-sí; **f** jāp;
g chīng-séui

3 a ga-fē-gā-náaih, jī-sí sāam-màhn-jih b chīng-séui; **c** pìhng-gwo-jāp, fó-téui-sā-lēut

Language discovery 2

Néih-séung yām-dī-mē nē?; Néih-séung sihk-dī-mē nē?; Juhng-yiu-dī-mē nē?

Practice 2

1 a sihk **b** yiu **c** yám
2 3 2 4 1

Speaking

You Yāt-būi pìhng-gwo-jāp, gāi-yuhk sāam-màhn-jih, ga-fē jáu-náaih;
Ngóh-séung yiu-būi chīng-séui, hon-bóu-bāau, tùhng-màaih ga-fē-ga-náaih.

Reading and writing

1 a jahp-choi-tōng, gāi-cháau-faahn, hùhng-dáu-sā, hēung-pín-chàah
b chēun-gyún, ga-lēi-gāi, baahk-choi, baahk-faahn, jī-màh-wú, hei-séui

Test yourself

1 a chā-siu **b** ga-lēi-gāi **c** gūk-fā (chrysanthemum tea)
2 Theo bē-jáu, hon-bóu-bāau; Kaia pìhng-gwó-jāp, fó-téui sāam-màhn-jih,
sīu-máaih

UNIT 8

Workaholics: Language discovery

lunch: ngaan-jau, **supper:** máahn-faahn

Vocabulary builder

daily routine: (finish) work, (get) up; **leisure time:** go to (the gym),
play (tennis), listen (to music)

Conversation 1

1 9 a.m. to 6 p.m.
2 a 4; **b** 5; **c** 6; **d** 2; **e** 3; **f** 1
3 a 7 a.m. **b** takes a shower, brushes teeth, washes face, and has breakfast
c goes home **d** reads the newspaper, surfs the internet, watches television

Language discovery 1

1 dím-yéung
2 (always) gīng-sèuhng; (usually) tūng-seuhng; (sometimes) yáuh-síh

Practice 2

1 a 3, **b** 4, **c** 2, **d** 1
2 a tái **b** dá **c** tēng **d** jouh
3 a, b & **d** Ngóh (your time) hai-sān/fāan-gūng/fong-gūng **c** Ngóh
(means of transportation) fāan-gūng.

Listen and understand

1 8.30 faan daai-hok 1.00 sik ngaan-jau 5.00 faan uk-kei
2 a pìhng-yāt **b** tūng-seung

Conversation 2

1 no
2 a 3 b 4 c 1 d 2
3 a F b F c F d F

Language discovery 2

1 **a** Ngóh-deih hóu-ngaan-ji héi-sān. **b** Pìhng-yāt bīn-go jyú-faahn nē? **c** Edmund wui tái-bou-jí.
2 **a** Bīn-go tēng-yām-ngohk? **b** Bīn-go séuhng-móhng?
3 **a** Kéuih hóu-ngaan ji fāan-ūk-kéih. **b** Kéuih hóu-ngaan ji jyú-faahn.
4 **a** Kéuih-deih wuíh hàahng-sāan. **b** Kéuih-deih wuíh dá-móhng-kàuh.

Practice 2

1 **a** wui **b** ji **c** bīn-go **d** ji
2 Gā-hòuh, Néih túhng-néih Barbara Sīng-kéih-luhk jouh-dī-mē ne?; Píng-yāt bīn-go jyú-faahn nē?; Gám, néih-deih ngaan-jau tūng-séung jouh-dī-mē ne?

Reading

a /漫畫家-1; **b** /聽音樂-4; **c** /行街睇戲-5; **d** She gets up at 7.30 every day. **e** on foot **f** goes shopping and watches movies with friends.

Test yourself

1 **a** fāan, fong **b** héi, chūng, yám; **c** sihk **d** Sihk, séuhng, tái
2 **a** 9 a.m. **b** aa-Wing goes to the gym; aa-Sam plays tennis; their son and daughter go hiking; **c** aa-Sam; **d** cinema

UNIT 9

Hobbies: Language discovery

ging (as in lùhng-jāu ging-douh) and choi (as in choi-máh)

Vocabulary builder

entertainment: movies
sports: football, cycling

Conversation 1

1 Frank; Shuk-ling
2 **a** Ngóh-hóu-chìh-ji héi-sān. **b** Ngóh heui-tái-hei. **c** Gám néih Sīng-kèih-luhk-yāt/jāu-muht jouh-mē aa? **d** Ngóh jīu-tàuh-jóu fāan-gūng. **e** Ngóh haih ūk-kéi duhk-Yīng-mán. **f** Ngóh dā-bīng-pōng-bō.
3 **a** hóu-chìh-héi-sān, m̀ouh-chēut-gāai, hai ūk-kéi duhk-Yīng-mán. **b** Jīu-tàuh-jóu fāan-gūng. Hah-jau tùng Issac dá yúh-móuh-kàuh. **c** chaai-dāan-chēd

Language discovery 1

1 a Ngóh móuh-chēut-gāai. **b** Ngóh duhk-Yīng-mán. **c** Ngóh-deih heui-tái-hei.

2 The verb forms remain unchanged regardless of subject, tense and anything else.

4 a Jūng-yi. **b** Neih-jūng-m̀h-jūng-yi dá bīng-pōng-bō? **c** Ngòh m̀h-jūng-yi tek-jyū-kàuh.

Practice 1

1 a pòuh **b** tái **c** heui **d** hàahng

2 a Tùhng Joshua hàahng-gūng-sī. **b** Dá yúh-móuh-káuh. **c** Cháai-dāan-chē tùhng yeh-pòuh. **d** Tùhng Grace heui-tái-hei. **e** Kàhm-yaht dá-làahm-kàuh. **f** (Jūng-yi) yeh-pòuh.

3 b Ngóh m̀h-jūng-yi tek-jūk-kàuh. **c** Ngóh jūng-yi dá-làahm-kàuh. **d** Ngóh m̀h-jūng-yi waaht-syut. **e** Ngóh hóu-jūng-yi yeh-pòuh. **f** Ngóh jūng-yi tái-hei.

4 Ngóh-tùhng pàhng-yáuh yeh-pòuh.; Ngóh hou-jūng-yi keuih.

Listen and understand

1 a hàang-gūng-sī **b** dá-làahm-kàuh **c** cháai-dāan-chē **d** tái-hei **e** heui-léuih-hàhng **f** dá-yúh-móuh-kàuh

2 a 3; **b** 2; **c** 3; **d** 1; **e** 3; **f** 2

Conversation 2

1 Yīng-gwok; Méih-gwok

2 a 3; **b** 5; **c** 1; **d** 2; **e** 4

3 a T; **b** T; **c** F; **d** F

Language discovery 2

1 a Ngóh (date) chēut-sai. **b** Ngóh (date) chēut-sai. **c** Ngóh yuh-dóu ngóh tai-tái. **d** Ngóh git(-jó)-fān. Give at least three phrases that indicate a past event. Any three of the following: gauh-nín (last year), kàhm-yaht (yesterday), chìhn-yaht (the day before yesterday), seuhng-chi (last time), ngāam-ngāam (just), tàuh-sīn (just now), yí-chìn (before).

Practice 2

1 4, 1, 2, 5, 3, 6;

2 a chēut-sai **b** duhk **c** yuh-dóu **d** git-fān

Speaking

a Ngóh (date of birth without year) sāang-yāt. **b** Ngóh (date of birth including year) chēut-sai. **c** Ngóh hái (place) chéut-sai. **d** Ngóh (year) hái daaih-hohk duhk-syu. **e** Ngóh (year) bāt-yihp. **f** Ngóh-hái (place/address) fāan-gūng.

Reading

2 Put down your name, gender, date of birth and place of birth.

Test yourself

1 a hàang **b** dá **c** tek **d** cháai
2 a 1st November 1977 **b** Happy Valley **c** bank manager **d** hotel manager

UNIT 10

Festivals: Language discovery

jit-yaht

Vocabulary builder

in the future: next (week); next (year)

Conversation 1

1 Oliver; Sophie
2 a 3, **b** 4, **c** 2, **d** 1
3 a It's Benjamin's birthday. **b** The Revolving Restaurant. It is cheaper, and provides a buffet, and therefore more choices of food.

Language discovery

1 a Néih gãm-máahn yáuh-mē gai-waahk? **b** Ngóh heui dá dihn-wá dehng-tói.;
Future events: tomorrow, the day after, tonight

Practice 1

1 a Edward hóu-faai wúi-heui Yīng-gwōk. **b** Báh-bā jéun-beih chēut-huei-sihk-faahn. **c** Diane dã-syun hah-Sīng-kèih-yāt hing-jūk sãang-yāt.
2 a Ge-fē beih cháh hóu-dī. **b** Ngh-sīng jáu-dīm beih leuhng-sīng jáu-dim gwaai-dī. **c** Faai-chāan-dim beih hōi-sīn jáu-gā pehng-dī.
d Gūng-gūng beih báh-bāa daaih-dī. **e** Sai-louh-jái beih pòh-pó sai-dī.
3 a 3; **b** 4; **c** 1; **d** 2
4 a Sān-nìhn ngóh jéun-beih . . . **b** Sing-daan-jit ngóh-wui . . . **c** Ngóh dá-syun heui . . . gwo-sãang-yāt.

Listen and understand

1 a S, **b** M, **c** M & H, **d** M & H, **e** H
2 a T, **b** F, **c** F, **d** T
3 Kim-hung-hóu; Yun-yi-gwaai; Kim-hung-sihk; Yun-yi-gwaai, sai, pèhng

Conversation 2

1 Lu-lu (accepts), Chi-ming (declines)
2 a 3, **b** 4, **c** 5, **d** 1, **e** 2
3 a Saturday **b** Lu-lu's university, 11.00 a.m. **c** is not well, has a cold

Practice 2

1 3, 5, 1, 4, 2
2 a Ngóh-m̀h-heui (sihk jih-jouh-chāan) yān-waih (hóu gwai). **b** Ngóh-
m̀h-heui (Hōi-sīn jáu-gā sihk-faahn) yān-waih (m̀h-hóu-sihk). **c** Ngóh-m̀h-
heui (néih ūk-kéi) yān-waih (hóu-mòhng). **d** Ngóh-m̀h-heui (party)
yān-waih (gám-mouh).
3 a dā-dihn-wá **b** Hing-jūk, bāt-yihp **c** bīn-douh **d** syū-fuhk.
4 The Revolving Restaurant (Syùhn-jyún cāan-tēng); she will be travelling.

Speaking

You Ngóh (gām-maahn) móuh-jit-muhk.; **You** Hóu-aa. (Néih-deih
dá-syun) heui bīn-douh sihk(-fāan) aa?; **You** Léuhng-gāan dōu-heui-gwo.
Hói-sīn jáu-gā béi-gauh gwai-dī, daahn-haih dī-yeh hóu-sihk dī.;
You Hóu-aa. Hái jáu-gā mùhn-háu dāng laa, hóu-m̀h-hóu aa?

Reading

date Wednesday 8th August; **time** 3 p.m.; **venue** my home

Test yourself

1 a 3, **b** 4, **c** 1, **d** 2
2 a gai-waahk **b** wui **c** séung **d** dá-syun
3 The Seafood Restaurant (Hói-sīn-jáu-gā); he has a cold.

Review 3

1 a fó-géi **b** heui-yám-chàh **c** chàh-lòuh **d** séui-sīn.
2 a hā-gáau **b** chēun-gyún **c** sīu-máaih **d** séui-sīn (chàh) **e** hei-séui
f hùhng-dauh-sā
3 a M̀h-gōi béi-go chāan-páai ngóh. **b** Néih séung sihk-dī-mē nē? **c** Ngóh
juhng-séung yiu-būi hùhng-jáu. **d** M̀h-gōi béi-dihp chēun-gyún ngóh.
e Néih-séung yám-dī mē nē? **f** Ngóh juhng-séung yiu-dī cháau-faahn.
4 a būi **b** dihp **c** jī **d** wún **e** wùh **f** lùhng
5 a Néih géi-dím fāan-gūng? **b** Néih dím-yéung fāan-gūng? **c** Néih
tūng-sèuhng gēi-dím heui gihn-sān-sāt gaa? **d** Néih géi-dím fong-gūng?
6 a sìh-sìh, gīng-sèuhng **b** pìhng-yāt **c** tùhng-séung **d** gaan-m̀h-jūng,
yáuh-sìh **e** chùhng-lòih m̀h-wui
7 a F, **b** T, **c** F, **d** T, **e** T

8 a jūng-yi **b** jeui jūng-yi **c** m̀h-jūng-yi **d** m̀h-jūng-yi **e** màh-má-déi
f jūng-yi
9 a Ngóh heui tái hei. **b** Ngóh hóu-jóu sihk jóu-chāan. **c** Ngóh jīu-tàuh-jóu/seuhng-jáu fāan-gūng. **d** Ngóh dāa-móhng-kàuh. **e** Néih (seuhng) jāu-muht/Sīng-kèih-lūk-yaht jouh-mē aa? **f** Ngóh hóu-chíh ji héi-sān.
10 a kàhm-yaht **b** seuhng-chi **c** gauh-nìhn **d** chìn-yaht **e** seuhng Sīng-kèih **f** tàuh-sīn
11 a 5, **b** 3, **c** 2, **d** 1, **e** 4
12 a Néih gēi-sìh sāang-yaht (gaa)? **b** Néih bīn-nìhn chēut-sai (gaa)?
c Néih hái bīn-douh jouh-yéh (gaa)? **d** Néih bīn-nìhn git-fān (gaa)?
e Néih hái bīn-douh cēut-sai (gaa)?
13 a 3, **b** 1, **c** 4, **d** 2
14 a next month **b** tomorrow **c** next year **d** the day after tomorrow
e tonight **f** next Tuesday
15 a heui **b** jéun-beih **c** wui **d** séung/dā-syun **e** dā-syun/séung **f** gai-waahk
16 a Hói-sīn béi-gaau gwaai-dī. **b** Dím-sām béi hói-sīn pèhng-dī. **c** Ngóh m̀h làih-dāk yān-waih ngóh-yáuh-dī gáam-mouh. **d** Jih-joh-chāan ge syún-jaahk béi-gaau dō-dī. **e** Cháang-jāp béi pìhng-gwo-jāp hóu-yám dī. **f** Ngóh-m̀h-séung sihk faahn yān-waih ngóh m̀h-tóuh-ngoh.

Cantonese–English vocabulary

Numbers in brackets indicate the unit in which the entry is introduced. Abbreviations:

cl	classifier
fp	final particle
ve	verb ending

aa	*softens the tone of a statement*	(1)
aa-	*prefix for names/relationships*	(1)
aa?	*fp: finishes a question*	(1)
āa	*fp: makes a reply sound polite or enthusiastic*	(1)
àah?	*fp: that's right, isn't it?*	(4)

bā-sí	*bus*	(4)
bā-sí-jaahm	*bus stop*	(4)
bā-sí-júng-jaahm	*bus terminus*	(6)
baahk-choi	*Chinese cabbage* (literally *white vegetable*)	(7)
baahk-faahn	*boiled/steamed rice*	(7)
baahk-jāu	*white wine*	(7)
baahk-sık	*white* (literally *white colour*)	(3)
baahn-gūng-sāt	*offices*	(8)
baak	*hundred*	(3)
baak-maahn	*a million*	(3)
bāan	*cl: group of, gang of*	(4)
baat	*eight*	(2)
baat-yuht	*August*	(5)
bāau	*include, wrap up*	(5)
bàh-bā	*father*	(2)
baih	*currency*	(3)
Bāk-gìng	*Beijing (Peking)*	(7)
Bāk-gìng-choi	*Peking food*	(7)
bān-gún	*guest house*	(5)
bāt-gwo	*but, however*	(9)
bāt-yihp	*graduation*	(10)
bē-jāu	*beer*	(7)
béi	*give*	(5)
béi-gaau	*compare, comparatively*	(10)
béi-go . . .	literally *give me a . . .*	(7)
bīn-douh?	*where?*	(6)
bīn-gāan?	*which one?*	(10)

bīn-go?	who? which one?	(2)
bīn-nìhn?	which year?	(9)
bīn-wái?	who?	(10)
bīn-yaht?	which date?	(4)
bīng-pōng-bō	table tennis; also **bīng-būmp-bō**	(9)
bok-maht-gún	museum	(6)
bou-jí	newspaper	(8)
buī	cup, glass	(7)
bun	half; also half an hour	(4)
bún-lòih	originally	(9)
bun-yé	after midnight (informal)	(4)
chāa-sīu	barbecue pork	(7)
chàahn-sou	floor	(6)
cháai-dāan-chē	cycling (literally step bicycle)	(9)
chāan-páai	menu	(7)
chāan-jau	table wine	(7)
chāan-tēng	restaurant	(10)
cháang-jāp	orange juice	(7)
cháang-sīk	orange (literally orange)	(3)
chaat-ngàh	brush teeth	(8)
cháau-faahn	fried rice	(7)
cháau-mihn	fried noodles	(7)
chàh	tea	(7)
cháh-chāan-tēng	Chinese-style café	(7)
cháh-lòuh	tea house	(7)
Chàhn	Chan (a surname)	(1)
chàm-yaht	yesterday; also **kàhm-yaht**	(9)
chāt	seven	(2)
chāt-yuht	July	(2)
Chek-laahp-gok	Chek Lap Kok (airport)	(4)
Chengdu	**Sìhng-dōu**, the capital of Sichuan province in South China	(4)
chéng	invite (short for **yīu-chéng**)	(10)
chéng	please	(5)
chéng-mahn	please may I ask (alternative of **chíng-mahn**)	(5)
chèuhng	long	(3)
chèuhng-dī	longer	(3)
chèuhng-fu	long trousers	(3)
chēun-kyún	spring roll	(7)
chēut-háu	exit	(4)
chēut-heui	go out	(10)
chēut-mihn/bihn	outside	(6)
chēut-nín	next year	(10)

chēut-sāang-deih-dím	*place of birth*	(9)
chēut-sāang-yaht-kèih	*date of birth*	(9)
chēut-sai	*born* (literally *come out to the world*)	(9)
chēut-tóu-mành-maht	*archaeological finds*	(6)
chìh	*late* (normally refers to time)	(9)
chìhn-mihn/bihn	*front*	(6)
chìhn-nín	*the year before last*	(9)
chìhn-yaht	*the day before yesterday*	(9)
Chìhng-yàhn-jit	*Valentine's Day*	(10)
chīm-méng	*sign, signature*	(5)
chīn	*thousand*	(3)
chín	*money*	(3)
chīng-séui	*tap water* (literally *clear water*)	(7)
chīng-fū	literally *address/call you*	(1)
chíng-mahn	*please may I ask* (alternative to **chéng-mahn**)	(1)
chīu-kǎp-síh-chèuhng	*supermarket*	(3)
chòhng	*bed*	(8)
choi	*food, cuisine; vegetables*	(7)
Bāk-gīng-choi	*Beijing food/cuisine*	(7)
Gwóng-dūng-choi	*Gwongdong food/cuisine*	(7)
Sei-cyūn-choi	*Sichuan food/cuisine*	(7)
Seuhng-hói-choi	*Shanghai food/cuisine*	(7)
choi-máh	*horse racing*; also **páau-máh** (*racehorses*)	(9)
Chùih	*Tsui* (a surname)	(1)
chùhng-lòih-m̀h-wúih	*never* (literally *ever never would*)	(8)
chùhng-lèuhng	*to take a bath/have a shower*	(8)
chýuhn-múhn	*completely full*	(5)
chyun	*spell*	(5)
dā	*play*, as in **dā làahm-kàuh** (literally *hit*)	(8)
dá-dihn-wá	*to make a phone call*	(10)
dā-móhng-kàuh	*play tennis*	(8)
dá-syun	*plan*	(10)
dá-syun	*intend*	(8)
daahn-haih	*but*	(6)
daai-jó	*take with, take along*	(3)
daaih	*big*	(3)
daaih-dī	*bigger*	(10)
daaih-gáam-ga	*sale*	(3)
Daaih-gwóng-chèuhng	*big square, Macau's Sanado Square*	(6)
daaih-hah	*building*	(6)
daaih-hohk	*university*	(2)
daaih-hohk-sāang	*university student*	(2)

daaih-jóu dī	a bit bigger	(3)
daaih-koi	about	(6)
daaih-máh	large (size)	(3)
daaih-pàih-dong	street stalls	(3)
Daaih-sām-bā-pàaih-fōng	the ruins of Macau's St Paul's Cathedral	(6)
dāan	single	(5)
dāan-chìhng fēi	single-trip ticket	(4)
dāan-yáhn-fóng	single room	(5)
daap	travel by	(4)
daih-	makes ordinal numbers	(6)
daih-yāt	the first	(6)
daih-yih	the second	(6)
dāk	can	(10)
dáng	wait	(10)
dāng	light	(10)
dāng-gei	booked-in, register	(5)
dehng	booking	(5)
dehng-fóng	book a room	(5)
dehng-fóng-jī-líu	room booking information	(5)
dehng-jó	have booked	(5)
dehng-tói	reserve a table	(10)
deih-dím	place, location	(2)
deih-(hah)-tit	MTR (short for **deih-hah-tit-louh**)	(4)
deih-hah-tit-louh	underground railway, MTR	(4)
deih-jāt-gūng-yún	Global Geopark of China	(6)
deih-jí	address	(6)
deih-kēui	area	(6)
deih-tit-jaahm	MTR station	(4)
deui	cl: *a pair of*	(3)
deui-m̀h-jyuh	sorry	(3)
deui-mihn	opposite	(6)
deui-mihn-haih . . .	opposite is . . .	(6)
dī	cl: *for plurals and uncountable things*	(7)
dihn-chè	tram	(4)
dihn-sih(-gèi)	television set	(8)
dinh-sih kehk	soap operas	(9)
dihn-wā	telephone	(5)
dihn-wá-houh mã	telephone number	(5)
dihn-yàuh	email	(5)
dihng, dihng-haih	or?	(3)
dihp	plate	(7)
dīk-sí	taxi	(4)
dím	short for **dím-jūng**; also *a point, spot, dot*	(4)
dím-bun	half past	(4)

dím-gáai	*why?*	(10)
dím-gáu	*a quarter to*	(4)
dím-jūng	*time* (literally *touch the clock*)	(4)
dím-sāam	*quarter past*	(4)
dím-sām	*dim sum* (small plate of snacks)	(7)
dím-sé	*how to write?*	(5)
dím(-yéung)	*how; in what way?*	(1)
dím-yéung?	*how to?*	(8)
dím(-yéung)-heui	*how to go*	(6)
dō-jeh	*thank you* (for things given)	(1)
dō-jeh-saai	*thank you very much*	(1)
dōu	*also*	(1)
dou	*arrive*	(4)
dou-daht	*arrive, arrival*	(5)
dōu-haih	*is/am/are also*	(2)
douh-hói-síu-lèuhn	*ferry* (crossing Victoria Harbour in Hong Kong)	(4)
duhk	*study* (literally *read*)	(2)
duhk-gán-syū	*studying*	(2)
duhk-sỳu	*study* (literally *read books*)	(9)
duhk-yùhn-syū	*finished studying*	(9)
Dūng-fōng-jī-jyū	*Pearl of the Orient* (fictional hotel name)	(5)
dyún	*short*	(3)
dyún-dī	*shorter*	(3)
faai-chāan-dim	*fast-food restaurant*	(8)
faai-sin	literally *express line* (for MTR etc.)	(4)
fāan-gūng	*go to work*	(2)
faat	*prosperous*	(2)
fān	*minutes* (short for **fān-jūng**), *separate*	(4)
fan-gaau	*sleep*	(8)
fān-géi	*telephone line extension*	(5)
fān-jūng	*minutes*	(4)
fēi	*ticket*	(4)
fēi-gēi, gēi	*aircraft, aeroplane*	(4)
fēi-gèi-chèuhng	*airport*	(4)
fēi-syun	*fast boat* (short for **pan-seh-fēi-syùhn**)	(4)
féih	*fat*	(3)
fó-chē	*railway train*	(4)
fó-chē-fēi	*train ticket*	(4)
fó-gei	traditional term for *waiter/waitress*	(7)
fó-téui	*ham*	(7)
fòhng-gāan, fóng	*room*	(5)
fong-gùng	*finish work*	(8)
fōng-heung	*direction*	(6)

fu	*trousers*	(3)
fuh-gahn	*nearby*	(6)
Fuhk-wuht-jit	*Easter*	(10)
fūi-sık	grey (literally *grey colour*)	(3)
fūng-séui	*feng-shui*	(5)
ga-fē	*coffee*	(7)
ga-fē-gā-náih	white coffee (literally *coffee with milk*)	(7)
ga-fē-jáu-náaih	black coffee (literally *coffee running away from milk*)	(7)
ga-fē-sīk, fē-sīk	brown (literally *brown colour*)	(3)
ga-lēi-gāi	*curried chicken*	(7)
gaa	fp: indicating emphasis or surprise	(8)
Gāa-hòuh	male name	(1)
gāai	*street*	(3)
gāai-bīn-dong	*street stalls*	(3)
gāai-gok	*street corner*	(6)
gāai-máih	*end of the street*	(6)
gāai-síh	*markets, wet-markets*	(6)
gaai-siuh	*introduce*	(1)
gaak-lèih	*next to*	(6)
gáam-ga	*lower the price*	(3)
gāan	cl: for houses and rooms	(5)
gaan-(m̀h-)jūng	*occasionally, sometimes*	(8)
gaau-syū	*teach*	(2)
gaau-tóng	*church*	(6)
gāau-tūng	*traffic, communication*	(4)
gāau-tūng-gūng-geuih	*transport*	(4)
gai-waahk	*a plan/to plan*	(10)
gāi-yuhk	*chicken (meat)*	(7)
gahn	*close to*	(6)
gám	*so, in that case*	(2)
gam	*so*	(7)
gám-àah	*is that so?*	(7)
gám-jauh	*if so*	(10)
gām-maahn	*tonight*	(10)
gām-máahn	*this evening, tonight*	(10)
gám-mouh	*a cold*	(10)
gām-yaht	*today*	(5)
gām-yaht-jīng-syún	*today's special*	(7)
gáu	*long-lasting*	(2)
gáu	*nine*	(2)
gáu-yuht	September	(5)

gauh	old (not new), used	(9)
gauh-nín	last year	(9)
ge	fp: that's how it is! (also see explanation in text)	(2)
gēi	short for **fēi-gēi**	(4)
géi	quite, rather, fairly	(1)
géi	several	(9)
géi?	how many? how much?	(3)
géi?	what	(9)
gēi-chèuhng	airport	(4)
gēi-chèuhng faai-sin	airport-express	(4)
géi-chín?	short for **géi-dō-chín**	(4)
géi-daaih (aa)?	How old? (literally how big?)	(2)
géi-dím?	short for **géi-dō-dím?**	(4)
géi-dō	how much? how many? (literally how a lot?)	(1)
géi-dō-chín?	How much money?	(3)
géi-dō-dím?	What time is it?	(4)
géi-dō-houh?	What is the number?	(5)
géi-go . . . ?	how many . . . ?	(2)
géi-houh?	short for **géi-dō-dím**	(5)
gei-jé	journalist	(2)
géi-lihm-yāt	anniversary	(10)
géi-máahn?	how many nights?	(5)
gēi-piu	air ticket	(5)
géi-sìh	what time?	(9)
gihn	cl: for most clothing items	(3)
gihn-sān-sāt	gym	(8)
Gim-kìuh	Cambridge	(4)
gin	see, meet	(10)
ging-douh	racing (literally race across)	(9)
gīng-léih	manager	(2)
gīng-sèuhng	always	(8)
git-fān	get married	(9)
giu	call, naming	(1)
go	cl: for people and many objects	(2)
gó	that	(3)
gó-bāan	that (train, bus, etc.)	(4)
gó-bihn	over there (literally that side)	(3)
gó-dī	those	(3)
gó-douh	there	(6)
gó-gihn	that piece of clothing	(3)
gó-jahn-sìh	then, at that time	(9)
gòh-gō	elder brother	(2)

Gong-baih, Góng-jí	*Hong Kong dollars*, also **Góng-yùhn**	(3)
góng-ga	*bargain*	(3)
gōu	*tall, high*	(2)
gū-lìhng	*loneliness*	(2)
gūk-fā	*chrysanthemum tea*	(7)
gūng-chìhng	*engineering*	(2)
gūng-gūng	*maternal grandpa*	(2)
gūng-jok	*work*	(2)
gūng-jok-kòhng	*workaholic*	(8)
gūng-ngaih-bán	*handicrafts*	(3)
gūng-yuh	*apartments*	(5)
gūng-yún	*park*	(9)
gwai	*expensive*	(10)
gwai-dī	*more expensive*	(10)
gwai-sing?	*what is your name?*	(1)
gwāt	*a quarter of an hour*	(4)
gwo-sāang-yāt	*celebrate one's birthday*	(10)
gwok(-gā)	*country, state*	(1)
gwóng-chèuhng	*square*	(6)
Gwóng-dūng	*Guangdong (province)*	(7)
Gwóng-dùng-choi	*Cantonese food*	(7)
Gwóng-dūng-wá	*language of Canton, Cantonese*	(1)
Gwóng-dūng-yahn	*Cantonese people*	(1)
Gwóng-jāu	*Guangzhou (Canton)*	(4)
Gwóng-jāu-wá	*language of Guangzhou, also Cantonese*	(1)
hā	*prawn, shrimp*	(7)
hā-gáau	*prawn dumpling*	(7)
hàahng	*to walk*	(3)
hàahng-gāai	*walk around* (literally *walking in the street*)	(3)
hàahng-gūng-sī	*window shopping*	(9)
hàahng-louh	*walk*	(8)
hàahng-sàan	*walk in the country, hiking*	(8)
hàaih	*shoe*	(3)
hāalo	*hello*	(1)
hah-go-yuht	*next month*	(10)
hah-jau	*afternoon, p.m.*	(9)
hah sīng-kèih	*next week*, also informal **hah-láih-baai**	(10)
hah-(yāt)-bāan	*next (train, bus, etc.)*	(4)
hah-(yāt)-chi	*next time*	(10)
hái	*at, in, on*	(2)
hái-bīn-(douh)?	*where?*	(2)
hái-gāai-máih	*at the end of the street*	(6)
hái-gaak-lèih	*next to*	(6)

hái-m̀h-hái-douh?	be . . . there? (literally be-not-be there?)	(10)
hái-nī-douh-hàhng-heui	walk from here	(6)
hái-nī-tìuh-gāai . . .	on this street	(6)
haih	be: is/am/are	(2)
haih-gám-dō?	is that all?	(7)
haih-gám-dō	that is all	(7)
haih-jó-bihn	on the left	(6)
haih-m̀h-haih?	is it?/are they? (literally be-not-be)	(2)
haih-yauh-bihn	on the right	(6)
hāk/hāak-sīk	black (literally black colour)	(3)
hauh-mihn/bihn	back	(6)
hauh-sāang	young (informal)	(2)
hauh-yaht	day after tomorrow	(10)
héi-gēui	one's everyday life at home	(8)
héi-sān	get up	(8)
héi-séui	soft drink	(7)
hei-yún	cinema	(6)
heui	go, go to	(4)
heui-bīn-douh?	where to go?	(10)
heui-gwo?	have (you) been?	(10)
heui-gwo	have been	(10)
heui-yám-chàh	have tea in a tea house (literally let's go drinking tea)	(7)
heung	towards	(6)
heung-chíhn-jau	go straight on	(6)
heung-chíhn-jihk-jáu	go straight on	(6)
Hēung-góng	Hong Kong	(1)
Hēung-góng-yàhn	Hong Kongers	(2)
hēung-pín	jasmine tea	(7)
hīng-daih	brothers (literally older and younger brothers)	(2)
hing-dín	celebration	(10)
hīng-jūk	to celebrate	(10)
hó-m̀h-hó-yíh?	may (I)? (literally can or cannot)	(3)
hó-ngaan	very late	(8)
hó-yíh	can	(3)
hōi	drive away, open	(4)
hói-déi seuih-douh	Cross Harbour Tunnel	(4)
hōi-mùhn	open (literally open door)	(8)
hōi-mùhn-sìh-gaan	opening time	(8)
Hói-sīn-jáu-gā	the Seafood Restaurant	(10)
hon-bóu-bāau	hamburger	(7)
hóu	good	(1)
hóu	very	(1)
hóu-di	better	(10)

hóu-gwai	*very expensive*	(3)
hóu-jūng-yi	*like (it) very much*	(9)
hóu-m̀h-hóu?	*Is it good?* (literally *good-not-good*)	(9)
hóu-sih-sihng-sēung	*good things come in pairs*	(2)
houh	*day of the month*	(4)
hùhng-dáu-sā	*red-bean soup*	(7)
hùhng-jau	*red wine*	(7)
hùhng-luhk-dāng	*traffic lights*	(6)
hùhng-sīk	*red* (literally *red colour*)	(3)
Hùhng-ham	*Hunghom* (place name)	(4)
hūng	*empty*	(5)
jaahm	*(bus, taxi, etc.) stop*	(4)
jaai	*vegetarian food*	(7)
jáan	*cl: for lamps and lights*	(6)
jahp-choi	*mixed vegetable*	(7)
jahp-choi-tōng	*mixed vegetable soup*	(7)
jái	*son*	(2)
jāk-bihn/mihn	*by the side; beside you*	(6)
jān-haih	*indeed*	(10)
jāp	*juice*	(7)
Jāu	*Chau* (a surname)	(1)
jáu	*wine, alcoholic drink*	(7)
baahk-jau	*white wine*	(7)
bē-jāu	*beer*	(7)
chāan-jau	*table wine*	(7)
hùhng-jau	*red wine*	(7)
jáu	*leave, run, run away*	(4)
jáu-dim	*hotel*	(5)
jáu-gā	*Chinese restaurant*	(7)
jáu-làuh	*Chinese restaurant*	(7)
jāu-muht	*weekend; also* **Sīng-keih-luhk-yaht**	(9)
jauh	*then, right away*	(8)
jauh-douh	*soon arrive*	(6)
jauh-haih	*that is*	(2)
jē	fp: *only, and that's all, no more than that*	(6)
jeui	*most*	(8)
jeui-jóu	*the earliest*	(4)
jéun-beih	*prepare; also* **yuh-beih**	(4)
Jeun-giht	male name	(1)
Jèung	*Cheung, Yeung* (a surname)	(1)
jēung	cl: for sheet-like objects	(4)
jèung-lòih	*future*	(10)
jī	cl: *(a) bottle (of); also* **jēun**	(7)

ji	*until then*	(8)
jī-hauh	*after*	(8)
jī-màh	*sesame*	(7)
jí-muih	*sisters* (literally *elder and younger sisters*)	(2)
jī-síh	*cheese*	(7)
ji-wáih	male name	(1)
jih	*characters; five minutes*	(4)
jih-jouh-chāan	*buffet*	(10)
jing-fú	*government*	(8)
jīng-syún	*special*	(7)
jip-doih-yùhn	*hotel receptionist*	(5)
jit-kau	*discount*	(3)
gáu-jit	*10% off*	(3)
baat-jit	*20% off*	(3)
chāt-jit	*30% off*	(3)
luhk-jit	*40% off*	(3)
ńgh-jit	*50% off*	(3)
sei-jit	*60% off*	(3)
sāam-jit	*70% off*	(3)
léuhng-jit	*80% off*	(3)
yāt-jit	*90% off*	(3)
jit-muhk	*programme, activity*	(10)
jit-yaht	*festival*	(10)
jīu-jóu	*morning*; also **jīu-tàuh-jóu**	(9)
jìuh	*Chiu* (a surname)	(1)
jó	ve: *completion*	(5)
jó-(sáu-)bihn	*left side*	(6)
joh	*flat* (also **sāt**)	(6)
joi	*again*	(10)
joih	*in*	(7)
Jóu-chāan	*breakfast*	(5)
jóu-sàhn	*good morning*	(1)
jouh	*do*	(8)
jouh-(dī-)mē?	short for **jou-māt-yéh?**	(8)
jouh-fāan	*early sleep*	(8)
jouh-jó-di-mē?	*what have (you) done?*	(9)
jouh-māt-yéh?	in context: *What do you for a living?*	(2)
	in general: *why? for what reason?*	
jouh-mē?	*What do you do?* (short for **jouh-māt-yéh**)	(8)
jouh-sinhg-hòhng	literally *What is your occupation?*	(2)
jouh-yéh	*work*	(2)
juhng	*still, yet*	(2)
juhng	*even more; furthermore*	(5)
juhng-séung	*still want; in addition, (I) would like . . .*	(3)

jūk-kàuh	*football, soccer*	(9)
Jūng-chāu-jit	*Mid-Autumn Festival*	(10)
Jūng-gwok	*China*	(1)
Jūng-gwok-chàh	*Chinese teas*	(7)
Jūng-gwok-yàhn	*a Chinese*	(2)
Jūng-gwok-yàuh	*travelling in China*	(4)
júng-guhng	*total*	(5)
jūng-hohk	*secondary school*	(2)
jūng-máh	*medium*	(3)
jūng-mán	*Chinese language* (informal)	(5)
jūng-màhn	*Chinese language*	(5)
jūng-m̀h-jūng-yi	*Do you like it?* (literally *like-not-like?*)	(9)
jūng-ńgh	*noon*	(4)
jūng-sām	*centre*	(6)
jūng-yi	*like, fond of*	(8)
jýu-choi	*main course*	(4)
jyú-faahn	*cook* (literally *cook rice*)	(8)
jyuh	*live*	(5)
jyuh-bīn-douh	*live where?*	(5)
jyun	*turn, change*	(6)
jyun-gok	*corner*	(6)
jyun-jó	*turn left*	(6)
jyun-yauh	*turn right*	(6)
kàhm-yaht	*yesterday;* also **chàhm-yaht**	(4)
káhn, or gáhn	*near, close to*	(6)
kau-maht syū-wùhn lìuh-faat	*retail therapy*	(3)
kèih-tà	*other*	(2)
kéuih	*he, she, it*	(1)
kéuih-deih	*they, them*	(1)
kwàhn	*dress, skirt*	(3)
lāa	fp: *as a matter of fact*	(1)
laa	fp: *that's how the case stands now*	(2)
laahm-chē	*tram* (short for **sān-dīng-laahm-chē**)	(4)
làahm-kàuh	*basketball*	(9)
làahm-sīk	*blue* (literally *blue colour*)	(3)
laaht	*spicy*	(7)
laak	fp: *that's how the case stands now*	(6)
làam-kàuh	*ruby*	(9)
lāang-sāam	*sweater*	(3)
làhm-yuhk	*shower*	(5)
làih	*come*	(4)

làih-dak	*can come*	(10)
Làuh	*Lau* (a surname)	(1)
Léih	*Li, Lee* (a surname)	(1)
lèih-dóu	*outlying island*	(6)
leng	*pretty, beautiful*	(2)
leng-jái	*handsome* (literally *handsome boy*; informal))	(2)
lèuhn-dou	*the turn of*	(5)
lèuhn-dou-léh	*your turn*	(5)
lèuhn-pún	*roulette*	(13)
léuhng	*two* (when followed by a classifier or noun)	(2)
leuih-biht	*type*	(5)
léuih-gún	*hostels*	(5)
léuih-hāak	*tourist*	(6)
léuih-hāak séun-maahn-jūng-sām	*Tourist Information Centre*	(6)
léuih-hàhng	*travelling*	(9)
lihk-sí	*history*	(2)
lìhng	*zero*	(2)
lìhng-dīng	*emptiness*	(2)
lìhng-sàhn	*midnight* (literally *zero morning*)	(4)
lohk	*alight, fall*	(2)
lòih-wùih fēi	*return ticket*	(4)
lóu	*flat*	(6)
lóuh-sī	*teacher*	(2)
luhk	*six*	(2)
luhk-yuht	*June*	(5)
lùhng	*bamboo basket for steaming dim sum*	(7)
lùhng-jāu	*dragon boat*	(9)
lùhng-jāu-ging-douh	*dragon boat race*	(9)
lùhng-lihk-sān-nìhn	*Chinese Lunar New Year*	(10)
maa?	fp: makes questions	(1)
máah-tàuh	*fragrant harbour*	(4)
máahn	*evening*	(5)
maahn	*ten thousand*	(3)
máahn-chāan	*supper, dinner*	(5)
máahn-faahn	*supper, dinner*	(8)
maahn-léih chèuhng-sìhng	*the Great Wall* (literally *ten-thousand-long-city*)	(4)
maahn-wá-gā	*cartoonist*	(8)
máaih	*buy*	(3)
maaih	*sell*	(3)
màaih-dāan	*make out the bill*	(4)
máaih-jó-keuih	*have bought it*	(3)
máaih-yéh	*shopping* (literally *buying things*; informal)	(3)

máh	*horse*	(9)
màh-jéuk	*mahjong* (literally *play sparrows*)	(9)
màh-mā	*mother*	(2)
màh-má	*paternal grandma*	(2)
mahn	*ask a question*	(5)
màhn-faa-gú-jīk	*cultural relics*	(6)
Màhn-móuh-míu	one of the first traditional-style temples built during British rule. Homage is paid to the Taoist gods of **Man** (literature) and **Mo** (war). The statues of **Baau-Gung** (god of justice), and **Sing-Wong** (god of the city) are also there.	(6)
màhn-yíh-sihk-wàih-tīn	*eating is heavenly*	(7)
maih	*kilometres*	(6)
mān	*dollar*	(3)
māt-yéh	*what? what kind of?*	(2)
mē	*what*; an alternative to **māt-yéh**	(1)
mē-méng?	literally *what name?*; an alternative to **māt-yéh-méng?**	(1)
mē-ngàan-sīk?	literally *What colour?*	(3)
Méih-gām, Méih-yùhn	*American dollars*	(5)
Méih-gwok	*USA*	(1)
m̀h	*not*	(2)
m̀h-faat	*not prosperous*	(2)
m̀h gán-yiu	*never mind, doesn't matter*	(2)
m̀h-gōi	*thank you* (for a service)	(1)
m̀h-gòi-màaih-dāan	*the bill please*	(7)
m̀h-gòi-néih	*excuse me*	(6)
m̀h-gòi-saai	*thank you very much*	(4)
m̀h-gòi . . . tim	*please . . . also*	(7)
m̀h-haih	*be not* (literally *not be*)	(2)
m̀h-sei	*not dying, no death*	(2)
míhn-fai	*free of charge*	(5)
mòhng	*busy*	(10)
móhng-kàuh	*tennis*	(8)
muhk	*wood*	(5)
mùhn-háu	*doorway, at the door*	(20)
mùih-múi	*sister*	(2)
nàahm-jōng	*clothes for men*	(3)
nàahm-pàhng-yáuh	*boyfriend*	(2)
nàahm-wàh-jóu-bou	*South China Morning Post*	(2)
nē?	fp: for rhetorical questions	(1)
nē?	fp: repeats same question	(1)
nēi-wái	*this is* (an alternative to **nī-wái**)	(1)
Néih-dēun-douh	*the main street in Kowloon Peninsula*	(6)

néih	*you*	(1)
néih-deih	*you* (plural)	(1)
néih-go	*yours*	(5)
néih-nē?	*What about you?*	(1)
néui	*daughter*	(2)
néuih-jong	*clothes for women*	(3)
néuih-pàhng-yáuh	*girlfriend*	(2)
néuih-sih	*Ms*	(1)
néuih-sih-ying	*waitress*	(7)
Ng	**Ǹgh** (a surname)	(1)
ngāam	*fit* (literally *correct*)	(3)
ngāam-m̀h-ngāam-san	*Does it fit?* (literally *fit or not fit?*)	(3)
ngāam-ngāam	*moment ago, just*	(9)
ngāam-san	*fit-well* (literally *fit body*)	(3)
ngaan	*late* (refers to *late in the day*)	(9)
ngaan-jau	*afternoon*	(8)
ngàahn-sīk	*colour*	(3)
ngàhn-hòhng	*bank*	(2)
ngái	*short, low*	(3)
ńgh	*five*	(2)
ńgh-chāan	*breakfast*	(5)
ńgh-on	*good afternoon*	(7)
ńgh-sihn	*lunch, lunch break*	(8)
ńgh-sīng-kāp	*five star, top class*	(5)
ńgh-yuht	*May*	(5)
ngóh	*I, me*	(1)
ngóh-deih	*we, us*	(1)
ngoih-tou	*jacket*	(11)
nī	*this*	(3)
nī-dī	*these*	(3)
nī-douh	*here*	(6)
nī-douh-hàahng-heui	*walk from here*	(6)
nī-gihn	*this piece of clothing*	(3)
nī-tìuh-gāai . . .	*this street*	(6)
nìhn-gēi	*age*	(2)
Ou-mún	*Macau*	(13)
paai-deui	*a party*	(10)
Páau-máh déi	*Happy Valley* (place name)	(6)
pàhng-yáuh	*friend*	(2)
pan-seh-fēi-syùhn	*turbojet*	(4)
pèhng	*cheap*	(3)
pèhng-dī	*cheaper*	(3)

pìhng-gwó-jāp	orange juice	(7)
pìhng-yaht	normally (literally normal days)	(8)
pòh-pó	maternal grandma	(2)
Póu-tùng-wá	Putonghua (Mandarin)	(1)
Pui-Lìhng	female name	(1)
sā	kind of thick soup, mainly for dessert	(7)
sá	practise (literally play as in **sá-taai-gihk**)	(9)
sā-lēut	salad	(7)
saai	ve: completely	(4)
sāam	three	(2)
sāam	clothing, shirt (short for **sēut-sāam**)	(3)
sāam-màhn-jih	sandwich	(7)
sāam-yuht	March	(5)
sāan-díng	Victoria Peak	(4)
saan-mùhn	close (literally close door)	(8)
sāang-chìh	new expression	(1)
sāang-yaht	birthday	(9)
sahp	ten	(2)
sahp-baat	eighteen	(2)
sahp-chāt	seventeen	(2)
sahp-cyùhn-saph-méih	perfect	(2)
sahp-gáu	nineteen	(2)
sahp-luhk	sixteen	(2)
sahp-maahn	a million	(3)
sahp-ńgh	fifteen	(2)
sahp-sāam	thirteen	(2)
sahp-sei	fourteen	(2)
sahp-yāt	eleven	(2)
sahp-yāt-yuht	November	(5)
sahp-yih	twelve	(2)
sahp-yih-yuht	December	(5)
sahp-yik	ten billion	(3)
sahp-yuht	October	(5)
sai	small	(3)
sai-di	smaller	(3)
sai-gihn-dī	smaller size clothing	(3)
sai-louh	children (short for **sai-louh-jái**)	(2)
sai-louh-jái	children	(2)
sai-máh	small (size)	(3)
sái-mihn	wash face	(8)
sái-sáu-gāan	toilet	(4)
sai-yāt-máh	a smaller size	(3)

Sāam-yih	female name	(1)
sān-mán	*news*	(9)
sau	*thin*	(3)
sáu-gēi	*mobile phone* (short for **sáu-tàih-dihn-wá**)	(5)
sáu-tàih-dihn-wá	*mobile phone*	(5)
sauh-fo-yùhn	*sales representative*	(3)
sauh-piu-yùhn	*person at the ticket office*	(4)
sé	*write*	(5)
séi	*die, dead*	(2)
sei	*four*	(2)
Sei-chỳun	*Sichuan (Szechwan)*	(7)
Sei-chỳun-choi	*Sichuan food*	(7)
sei-yuht	*April*	(5)
seuhng	*last*	(4)
séuhng-chòhng	*go to bed*	(8)
seuhng-go-yuht	*last month*	(9)
Seuhng-hói	*Shanghai*	(4)
Seuhng-hói-choi	*Shanghai food/cuisine*	(7)
seuhng-jau	*morning, a.m.*	(4)
séuhng-móhng	*surf the internet*	(8)
Seuhng sīng-kèih	*last week*	(9)
seuhng-(yāt)-bāan	*next (train, bus, etc.)*	(4)
seuhng-(yāt)-chi	*last time*	(9)
seui	*year of age*	(2)
séui-sīn	*narcissus tea*	(7)
séun-maahn	*enquiry*	(6)
sēung	*double*	(5)
séung	*would like to* (literally *want; like to have*)	(3)
sēung-chèhng	*shopping malls*	(3)
sēung-muh-làhm	a description of how the surname Lam is written	(5)
sēung-yàhn-fóng	*double room*	(5)
séung-yiu	*would like to have* (literally *want to have*)	(3)
sēut-sāam	*shirt*	(3)
si-hou	*hobby*	(9)
sī-sān	*try on*	(3)
sī-sān-sāt	*fitting room*	(3)
sih	*key*	(5)
sih-gaan	*time*	(4)
sih-gāan	*time*	(5)
sih-sih	*always*	(8)
sihk	*eat*	(7)
sihk-fahn	*having meals* (literally *eat rice*)	(8)
sihk-jóu-chāan	*have breakfast*	(8)

sihk-maahn-fahn	*have supper*	(8)
sihk-maht	*food*	(3)
sihk ngaan-jau	*have lunch* (literally *eat afternoon*)	(8)
sīn-sāang	*teacher* (informal)	(2)
sīn-sāang	*Mr*	(1)
sīn-sāang	*husband*	(2)
sing	*surname*	(1)
sing-biht	*gender*	(9)
Sing-daan-jit	*Christmas*	(10)
Sīng-gwōng-daaih-douh	*the Avenue of Stars*	(6)
sīng-kèih	*week*	(4)
sīng-kèih-yāt	*Monday*	(4)
sīng-kèih-jih	*Tuesday*	(4)
sīng-kèih-sāam	*Wednesday*	(4)
sīng-kèih-sei	*Thursday*	(4)
sīng-kèih-ńgh	*Friday*	(4)
sīng-kèih-luhk	*Saturday*	(4)
sīng-kèih-yaht	*Sunday*	(4)
sīng-kèih-luhk-yaht	*Saturday & Sunday*	(9)
sing-mìhng	*name*	(5)
síu	*few, little*	(4)
síu-bā	*minibus, light bus*	(4)
sīu-hín	*pastime; leisure*	(8)
síu-jé	*Miss*	(1)
síu-lèuhn	*ferry* (short for **douh-hói-síu-lèuhn**)	(4)
sīu-máai	*pork and shrimp dumplings*	(7)
sō-hòuh	a lively dining district in the west of Hong Kong Island (short for *South of Hollywood Road*)	(6)
sóu-sìh	key	(5)
suhk-fan	female name	(1)
syū-faat	*calligraphy*	(9)
sỳu-fuhk	*comfortable*	(10)
syùhn-jyun-cāan-tēng	*the Revolving Restaurant*	(10)
syún-jaahk	*choices*	(10)
syut-gōu	*ice cream*	(7)
taai	*too much*	(3)
taai-chèuhng	*too long*	(3)
taai-daai	*too big*	(3)
taai-dyún	*too short*	(3)
taai-gihk	*tai-chi*; also **taai-gihk-kyùhn**	(9)
taai-gwai	*too expensive*	(3)

taai-táai	Mrs	(1)
taai-táai	wife	(2)
tái	look at	(5)
tái-hah	a quick look (literally look down)	(5)
tái-hei	see a play, go to the cinema (literally watch a film)	(8)
tái-lohk	look as though	(2)
tàih-mahn	ask, questioning	(3)
tàuh-pùhn	starter	(7)
tàuh-sìn	just now	(9)
tek	kick	(9)
tēng	listen	(8)
tīm	fp: as well, what's more, also	(2)
tīng-yaht	tomorrow	(10)
tìuh	cl: for long flexible things	(3)
tòng	soup	(7)
tou	cl: set of, suit of	(5)
tou-chāan	set dinner	(7)
tou-fóng	en suite	(5)
tòuh-syū-gún	library	(8)
tùhng	with, and (short for **tùhng-màaih**)	(8)
Tuhng-lòh-wāan	Causeway Bay on Hong Kong Island	(6)
tùhng-màaih	and	(2)
tūng-sèuhng	usually	(8)
uūk-kéi	home	(8)
wá	language, speech	(1)
Wāan-jái	a district on Hong Kong Island	(6)
waahk-jé	or, perhaps	(8)
waaht-syut	skiing	(9)
Wàh-Mèih-Laih	a fictional hotel name	(6)
wahn-duhng	physical exercise	(8)
wàhn-tān-mihn	won-ton noodles	(7)
wái!	hello! (on the phone)	(4)
wàih-chyūn	village	(6)
wán	look for	(10)
wíhng	forever	(2)
wo	fp: to express recognition with slight surprise	(2)
Wòhng	Wong (a surname)	(1)
wòhng-sīk	yellow (literally yellow colour)	(3)
wú	kind of thick soup, usually for dessert	(7)
wùh	pot; **yāt-wùh** a pot of	(7)

wuh-lỳuhn-móhng	*internet*	(5)
wuh-sih	*nurse*	(2)
wúih	*able to; shall/will*	(4)
wún	*bowl*	(7)
Yàhn-màhn-baih	*Renminbi, RMB* (the currency of the PRC)	(3)
yahp	*enter*	(4)
yahp-háu	*entrance*	(4)
yahp-mihn/bihn	*inside*	(6)
yaht	*day*	(5)
yaht-kèih	*day of the month*	(5)
yám	*drink*	(7)
yám-bán	*drinks*	(7)
yām-ngohk	*music*	(8)
yān-waih	*because*	(10)
yāt	*one*	(2)
yāt-chàih	*together*	(10)
yat-sèuhng	*daily, everyday*	(8)
yat-sèuhng-héi-gēui	*daily routine*	(8)
Yāt-yuht	*January*	(5)
yauh	*furthermore, also*	(3)
yáuh	*have*	(2)
yáuh-dī	*some, a little bit*	(10)
yàuh-láahm	*sight seeing*	(6)
yáuh-móuh	*do (you) have* (literally *have-not*)	(3)
yauh-(sáu-)bihn	*right side*	(6)
yàuh-séui	*swimming*	(9)
yáuh-sìh (hauh)	*sometimes*	(8)
yéh	*thing, object*	(1)
yeh	*night*	(8)
yeh	*late* (refers to *late at night*)	(9)
yeh-fan	*sleep late*	(8)
yeh-máahn	*night-time*	(4)
yeh-pòuh	*clubbing*	(9)
yèh-yé	*maternal grandpa*	(2)
yeuhk-fòhng	*chemist's*	(6)
yi-chìhn	*before*	(9)
yī-fuhk	*clothes*	(3)
yī-sāng	*doctor*	(2)
yī-yún	*hospital*	(2)
yih	*two*	(2)
yìh-ché	*moreover*	(10)
yìh-gā	*now*	(4)

yíh-gìng	*already*	(4)
yih-saph	*twenty*	(2)
yih-saph-yāt	*twenty-one*	(2)
yih-saph-yih	*twenty-two*	(2)
yih-saph-sāam	*twenty-three*	(2)
yih-saph-sei	*twenty-four*	(2)
yih-saph-ńgh	*twenty-five*	(2)
yih-saph-luhk	*twenty-six*	(2)
yih-saph-chāt	*twenty-seven*	(2)
yih-saph-baat	*twenty-eight*	(2)
yih-saph-gáu	*twenty-nine*	(2)
yih-yuht	*February*	(5)
yìhn-hauh	*afterwards*	(8)
yìhng-yuhng-chìh	*descriptive words; adjectives*	(2)
yīk	*hundred million*	(3)
Yīng-gwok	*UK*	(1)
yiu	*want*	(3)
yìu-chéng	*to invite*	(10)
yiu-yáuh	*literally must have*	(5)
yuh-dehng	*reservation*	(5)
yuh-dóu	*meet*	(9)
yùh-lohk	*entertainment*	(9)
yúh-móuh-kàuh	*badminton*	(9)
yuhk	*meat*	(7)
yuhk-sāt	*bathroom*	(5)
yùhn	*dollar*	(7)
yùhn	*finished, completed*	(8)
yúhn	*far, distant*	(6)
yùhn-sīu	*the fifteenth day of the new year, the Spring Lantern Festival*	(10)
yuht, yuht-fahn	*moon, month*	(5)
yat-yuht	*January*	(5)
yih-yuht	*February*	(5)
sāam-yuht	*March*	(5)
sei-yuht	*April*	(5)
ńgh-yuht	*May*	(5)
luhk-yuht	*June*	(5)
chāt-yuht	*July*	(5)
baat-yuht	*August*	(5)
gáu-yuht	*September*	(5)
sahp-yuht	*October*	(5)
sahp-yāt-yuht	*November*	(5)
sahp-yih-yuht	*December*	(5)

VOICE CREDITS:

Recorded at Alchemy Studios, London

Cast: Xiao Lan Deng, Maisy Luk, Oscar Kwan, Waipang Sham, Katherine Pageon